Making the Law Work for Everyone

VOLUME I

Report of the Commission on Legal Empowerment of the Poor

FSC

Mixed Sources

Product group from well-managed forests, controlled sources and recycled wood or fiber

Cert no. SW-COC-001734
www.fsc.org
© 1996 Forest Stewardship Council

ISBN: 978-92-1-126219-3

Printed in the U.S.A. by Toppan Printing Company America Inc. (New Jersey), a company that is both ISO 14001:2004 and Forest Stewardship Council (FSC) certified for Environment and ISO 9001:2000 for Quality. Paper used is process chlorine free, acid free, 10 % recycled post-consumer waste and Forest Stewardship Council certified. All inks used are low VOC and vegetable-based.

Foreword

In New York last July, the UN Secretary General Ban Ki-moon and I spoke of the need to encourage the international community to accelerate progress on the Millennium Development Goals. The Call to Action focuses on mobilising not just governments but also the private sector, NGOs, civil society and the faith community to do more to achieve the Millennium Development Goals. The UK government will continue to push forward the need for accelerated action at every possible opportunity in 2008, including through its roles in the G8 and the European Union.

Making the Law Work for Everyone examines issues that will have a profound influence on human potential and progress towards the Millennium Development Goals. Three years ago, a distinguished group of scholars, former heads of state, senior policy makers and thinkers came together to explore the issue of legal empowerment of the poor.

I want to applaud my former colleagues' final product. I agree with the overall finding that by expanding and deepening universal legal protection, poor people will be better able to free themselves from poverty.

As the Report highlights, the sources of legal exclusion are numerous and very often country-specific. However, four common threads stand out. First, legal empowerment is impossible when poor people are denied access to a well-functioning justice system. Second, most of the world's poor lack effective property rights and the intrinsic economic power of their property remains untapped. Third, poor people, in particular women and children, suffer unsafe working conditions because their employers often operate outside the formal legal system. Fourth, poor people are denied economic opportunities as their property and businesses are not legally recognised. They cannot access credit, investment nor global and local markets.

The UK government is committed to working to reduce poverty and vulnerability amongst the world's poor by providing aid to developing nations and championing issues such as debt relief. We are collaborating with partners to provide advice to governments and donor agencies on policies that facilitate the participation of poor people in economic growth and that have an impact on poverty reduction. This Report, a product of research, analysis and consultations in more than

20 developing countries by international experts and staff will stimulate debate and discussions that have a profound bearing on progress towards achieving the Millennium Development Goals.

Concretely we are more than half way from 2000 to 2015. Yet, in reality we are still a million miles away from success. Earlier this year, UN Secretary General Ban Ki-moon labelled 2008 as the year of the "bottom billion" – a year for critical action on the MDGs. *Making the Law Work for Everyone* provides a needed and valuable voice for structural changes that will provide the poor a valuable tool as they work to pull themselves from the grips of poverty.

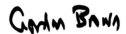

Gordon Brown
Prime Minister of the United Kingdom
Former Member of the Commission

Preface

In November 2006, a delegation from the Commission on Legal Empowerment of the Poor visited a teeming open air market (known as the 'Toi market') in an impoverished neighborhood in Nairobi, Kenya. To picture the market, imagine a mall without walls – or, for that matter, a roof or a floor – where each business is represented by a small table or a blanket laid on the ground. Imagine, as well, a surrounding area that is notorious for poor sanitation, pollution and crime. Floods are frequent. About one person in five has HIV/AIDS. Most of the residents lack legal title to the ramshackle dwellings they call home or to the tiny businesses upon which they depend for a living. These are men and women who are vulnerable and disadvantaged in every way – except for one – they are determined not to be victims.

About a decade ago, the sellers in the market created a communal savings plan to which each contributed fifteen cents a day. The money was used for small business loans and to make civic improvements, such as a public bath. Fifteen cents a day may seem a trifling sum, but in that place and for those people the payment often meant forgoing the purchase of new clothes for a child, food for the family, or a used bicycle for transportation. This was democracy at its purest – the willing surrender of a private benefit to build a ladder out of poverty for the community as a whole. Proposals for loans and projects were approved openly and collectively, with consent signified by the wiggling of fingers and the clapping of hands. Over time, the fund grew by tiny increments to more than $200,000.

This was still not much in a market with 5000 stalls crammed together, selling everything from toys and cabbage and to spark plugs and flip-flops. Still, the savings plan was a source of hope and pride to people who had put their faith in cooperative action, understood the importance of abiding by shared rules, and were doing everything possible to help themselves. Their courage underlined our conviction that those who consider poverty to be just another part of the human condition are ignorant, for the poor do not accept it, and when given the chance, will seize the opportunity to transform their lives. Because of what we saw and the people we met, the Commission left Nairobi encouraged.

Then, in December 2007, Kenya held a presidential election. The voting was flawed and fights broke out. Hundreds of people died and the market we visited was completely destroyed. There is literally nothing left.

In reply to its expression of sorrow and concern, the Commission received a letter from Joseph Muturi, one of the market leaders. He wrote that the social fabric built up over decades had been torn, and that people had been forced into exile in their own country, simply because of their ethnicity. 'We have gone back in time,' he wrote, and 'it will take us many years to come back to the level where we were both socially and economically.' He observed that it had taken Kenyans to make Kenya; and now Kenyans had broken Kenya; but they would – he was sure – recover it again, although at an expense of time and resources that could never fully be regained.

The lesson is clear. When democratic rules are ignored and there is no law capable of providing shelter, the people who suffer most are those who can least afford to lose. Creating an infrastructure of laws, rights, enforcement, and adjudication is not an academic project, of interest to political scientists and social engineers. The establishment of such institutions can spell the difference between vulnerability and security, desperation and dignity for hundreds of millions of our fellow human beings.

In his letter from the ruins of the Toi market, Joseph Muturi said that 'the big task that has occupied me is to try to bring the people together in order to salvage our sense of community.' Creating a sense of mutual responsibility and community on a global basis is a key to fighting poverty and a challenge to us all. It is our hope that this Commission report, with its recommendations, will help point the way to that goal and to a better and more equitable future for us all.

Respectfully,

Madeleine K. Albright   Hernando de Soto

Co-Chairs
Commission on Legal Empowerment of the Poor

Acknowledgements

A task of this magnitude and complexity can only be successfully accomplished by the invaluable contributions of people with a wide array of expertise and skills. This report is the outcome of much deliberation among the Commission members. While they had many different views, some of which might still persist, we are delighted by the convergence of opinion that occurred during our final meeting, leading to the consensus that we now present.

The report benefited greatly from the guidance and intellectual support provided by the members of the Commission's Advisory Board and we gratefully acknowledge their contributions. We thank the chairs, rapporteurs, and members of the working groups who provided an analytical and knowledge base. Their work, in the form of five working group reports, is presented in Volume II of the report of the Commission. The individual contributors to the working group reports are acknowledged in Volume II.

We are grateful to the national and local authorities, too many to mention, who were responsible for the successful conduct of the national consultations in 22 countries around the world.

We extend special thanks to the donors who have made generous contributions to the work of the Commission: Canada, Denmark, Finland, Iceland, Norway, Sweden, Switzerland, Ireland, Spain, the United Kingdom, the African Development Bank and the European Commission.

We recognise the host institution, the United Nations Development Program (UNDP), and especially Olav Kjørven for his leadership role, as well as Maaike de Langen and Hugh Roberts who tirelessly contributed to the drafting of the report. Furthermore, we extend our gratitude to all those UNDP Country Offices that supported the national consultations.

Mona Brøther, on behalf of the Government of Norway played a special role in co-ordinating the donors and in making substantive contributions to our work. Joseph Muturi deserves special mention for his work that inspired the Commission. We are grateful to Commission Member Allan Larsson for his contribution to early drafts of the report, and to Philip Legrain, Tim Mahoney and Francis Cheneval for contributions to various stages of the drafting process.

Special thanks also go to the Commission support team composed of the Secretariat whose present and former staff includes Cate Ambrose, Martha Barrientos, Ove Bjerregaard, Timothy Dolan, Jill Hannon, Sid Kane, Shara Kaplan,

Paulina Kubiak, Mala Mathur, Parastoo Mesri, Adriana Ruiz-Restrepo, Shomwa Shamapande, Harsh Singh, Veronique Verbruggen, and Nu Nu Win, as well as to the staff of the co-chairs, especially Kristin Cullison and Gabriel Daly. They all provided painstaking support to the multifaceted operational demands of the Commission, as well as the drafting and editing of the report.

A long list of interns and volunteers supported the Commission, including Sabiha Ahmed, Shailly Barnes, Camilo Alejandro Barrera, Wanning Chu, Francesco Di Stefano, Fabio Gonzalez Florez, Patricia de Haan, Mario Daniel Gómez, Ruth Guevara, Alena Herklotz, Brian Honermann, Emily Key, Rajju Malla-Dhakal, Diego Felipe Otero,Farzana Ramzan, Alec Schierenbeck, Erica Salerno, Asrat Tesfayesus, Sebastián Torres Luis Villanueva, and Tara Zapp.

Last but not least, we thank Jean-Luc Fiévet for generously contributing several photographs for inclusion into the report and Cynthia Spence for design and layout of this publication.

Madeleine K. Albright	Naresh C. Singh	Hernando de Soto
Co-Chair	Executive Director	Co-Chair

The Commission

Co-Chairs

Madeleine K. Albright is the former United States Secretary of State and the former U.S. Permanent Representative to the United Nations. She is currently a Principal of The Albright Group LLC and Chair and Principal of Albright Capital Management LLC, an investment advisory firm focused on emerging markets.

Hernando de Soto is President of the Institute for Liberty and Democracy and author of the seminal works *The Mystery of Capital* and *The Other Path*.

Executive Director

Naresh C. Singh is Director General of Governance and Social Development at the Canadian International Development Agency (on leave) and the former Principal Adviser on Poverty and Sustainable Livelihoods at UNDP.

Commission Members

Fazle Hasan Abed is the founder and chairperson of BRAC, one of the world's largest Development organizations based in Bangladesh.

Lloyd Axworthy is the current President and Vice-Chancellor of the University of Winnipeg. He is the former Foreign Minister of Canada (1996 to 2000) and currently serves on the board of the MacArthur Foundation, Human Rights Watch, Pacific Council, and others.

El Hassan bin Talal is committed to building societies in which people can live and work in freedom and with dignity. He is the President of the Arab Thought Forum and is currently working on the construction of a citizens' charter and a social charter to embody a code of ethics and to promote societal development in the West Asia North Africa region.

Fernando Henrique Cardoso is the former President of Brazil (1995 to 2002) and the former president of the Club of Madrid (2003 to 2006).

Shirin Ebadi is an Iranian lawyer and human rights activist, who received the Nobel Peace Prize in 2003.

Ashraf Ghani is the Chairman of the Institute for State Effectiveness and is the former Minister of Finance, Afghanistan.

Medhat Hassanein is Professor of Banking and Finance with the Management Department of the School of Business, Economics and Communication at the American University in Cairo and was formerly the Minister of Finance, Egypt.

Hilde Frafjord Johnson is the former Minister of International Development of Norway and Member of Parliament, having served over two government tenures, the first also as Minister of Human Rights. In a different capacity, Ms. Johnson is currently the Deputy Executive Director in UNICEF.

Anthony McLeod Kennedy is an Associate Justice of the Supreme Court of the United States of America. Throughout his legal career he has taught law, and for many years has taught in Europe on the subject of fundamental rights.

Allan Larsson is a former Finance Minister of Sweden and a former Member of the Swedish Parliament. He also served as Director General of the Swedish National Labour Market Board and as Director-General in the EU Commission. He is currently a chairman of Lund University and adviser to the President of the EU Commission on energy and climate change.

Clotilde Aniouvi Médégan Nougbodé is the President of the High Court of Benin. She was formerly the Director of Cabinet of the Minister of Justice and Legislation, Benin and founding member of the Benin Association of Law Practitioning Women (AFJB), a nonprofit organization.

Benjamin Mkapa is the former President of Tanzania. He is currently a Chairman of the South Centre, a Co-Chair of the Investment Climate Facility for Africa and an active player in peace negotiations in the Great Lakes Region of Africa.

Mike Moore is the former Prime Minister of New Zealand and the former Director-General of the World Trade Organization (1999 to 2002). He is active on a number of commercial boards and universities and was also a member of the UN Commission on International Migration.

Milinda Moragoda is a former Minister for Economic Reforms, Science and Technology and the former Deputy Minister for Plan and Implementation in Sri Lanka. He currently serves as the Minister of Tourism.

S. Tanwir H. Naqvi retired from the Pakistan Army in the rank of Lieutenant General in December 1995 and served as Federal Minister in the capacity of Chairman, National Reconstruction Bureau, an organization he founded and led for three years (1999 to 2002) for re-structuring the governance institutions of Pakistan to make them responsive to the demands of the 21st Century.

Mary Robinson is the former President of Ireland and the former United Nations High Commissioner for Human Rights. She is currently the President of Realizing Rights: The Ethical Globalization Initiative (EGI).

Arjun Sengupta is a former Professor at the School of International Studies, Jawaharlal Nehru University and an Adjunct Professor at the Harvard School of Public Health. He is currently Chairman of the Centre for Development and Human Rights in New Delhi and Chairperson of the UN Inter-governmental Working Group on the Right to Development in Geneva. He is also a Member of the Indian Parliament.

Lindiwe Sisulu is currently the Minister of Housing and a Member of Parliament of the Republic of South Africa.

Lawrence H. Summers is the former President of Harvard University and the former United States Secretary of the Treasury. He currently serves as a managing director of D.E. Shaw, an alternative investment firm.

Erna Witoelar is the former Minister of Human Settlements and Regional Development and member of the National Assembly of Indonesia. She was the UN special Ambassador for MDGs in Asia & the Pacific until the end of 2007 and is currently on several governing boards of CSOs working on sustainable development and governance reform.

Ernesto Zedillo is the former President of Mexico and is currently the Director of the Center for the Study of Globalization, Professor in the Field of International Economics and Politics and Professor Adjunct of Forestry and Environmental Studies at Yale University.

Members of the Advisory Board

Robert Annibale, Global Director of Microfinance, Citigroup

Marek Belka, Executive Secretary, United Nations Economic Commission for Europe (UNECE)

Diego Hidalgo, Founder, Club of Madrid

Donald Kaberuka, President, African Development Bank Group

Jean Lemierre, President, European Bank for Reconstruction and Development

Louis Michel, Commissioner for Development and Humanitarian Aid, European Commission

Luis Alberto Moreno, President, Inter-American Development Bank

Kumi Naidoo, Secretary-General and CEO, CIVICUS

Sheela Patel, Founding Director, Society for the Promotion of Area Resources (SPARC)

Jan Peterson, Founder and Chair, Huairou Commission

Juan Somavia, Director-General, International Labour Organization

Anna Tibaijuka, Executive Director, UN HABITAT

Victoria Tauli-Corpuz, Chairperson, UN Permanent Forum on Indigenous Issues

John Watson, Former President, CARE Canada

Francisco Garza Zambrano, President, Cemex North America

Robert Zoellick, President, World Bank

Table of Contents

This is the first of two volumes of the work of the Commission. The second volume is published separately (available at www.undp.org/legalempowerment) and consists of the outcomes of five working groups established to inform the Commission's deliberations. There may be instances in which the messages in this report go beyond those of the working groups in volume II.

In the 21ˢᵗ century, legal
four billion excluded is the
energies needed to enc
stable and peaceful world.

Executive Summary

empowerment of the
key to unlocking vital
poverty and build a more

The spectre of poverty and the resultant suffering from want and fear have been realities for so long that poverty is often deemed to be a natural and inevitable part of the human condition. In earlier times, when the struggle merely to survive was paramount for most people, this conclusion seemed reasonable, perhaps even unavoidable. In our era, however, we have every possibility to make economic opportunity broadly available. In the last six decades, more wealth has been created than in all previous history. No longer can it be argued that poverty is natural or inevitable.

Though many have shared in this prosperity, far too many of the world's people have been left behind, still living in deprivation, taking talent unused to the grave. Sub-Saharan Africa is not on track to achieve any of the Millennium Development Goals and extreme poverty persists on every continent. Statistics abound of the number of people that live in extreme income poverty, no matter how hard they work. And lack of income is just one dimension of poverty.

This Commission argues that four billion people around the world are robbed of the chance to better their lives and climb out of poverty, because they are excluded from the rule of law.[1] Whether living below or slightly above the poverty line, these men, women, and children lack the protections and rights afforded by the law. They may be citizens of the country in which they live, but their resources, modest at best, can neither be properly protected nor leveraged. Thus it is not the absence of assets or lack of work that holds them back, but the fact that the assets and work are insecure, unprotected, and far less productive than they might be. There are further vulnerabilities, as well. Indigenous communities may be deprived of a political voice and their human rights violated. In addition to exclusion based on their poverty and their gender, poor women may also be denied the right to inherit property. In our own era then, vast poverty must be understood as created by society itself.

In too many countries, the laws, institutions, and policies governing economic, social, and political affairs deny a large part of society the chance to participate on equal terms. The rules of the game are unfair. This is not only morally unacceptable; it stunts economic development and can readily undermine stability and security. The outcomes of governance – that is, the cumulative effect of policies and institutions on peoples' lives – will only change if the processes of governance are fundamentally changed.

The Commission...

The Commission on Legal Empowerment of the Poor was created to address this challenge. It is comprised of 21 Commissioners, including former heads of state and government, cabinet ministers, jurists, economic researchers, and other senior policymakers from the North, South, East and West. We hold diverse views regarding the pluses and minuses of globalisation but agree on the imperative of finding better ways to fight poverty and exclusion. During the past three years, we conducted 22 national consultation processes with representatives from local governments, academia, civil society, and grassroots movements. We launched five technical working groups, which submitted specialised reports. We drew on our own experience, reviewed relevant literature, talked to people from all walks of life, and debated with national and international policymakers and amongst ourselves. We have seen

and heard success stories, and we believe there is compelling evidence that when poor people are accorded the protections of the rule of law, they can prosper.

... and its Assessment: Four Billion Lives Excluded

The Commission believes poverty is manmade, by action and inaction, and a failure of public policies and of markets. The Commission sees that in rich countries people are more likely to enjoy access to justice and other rights – as workers, businesspeople, and owners of property. The recent, and vast, creation of wealth rests upon various legal protections, norms, and instruments governing such things as business organisations, corporations, tradable assets, labour contracts, workers associations, venture capital, insurance, and intellectual property. While the same protections and instruments exist in many developing countries, the overwhelming majority has no way to access them. Notwithstanding this reality, the legal underpinnings of entrepreneurship, employment, and market interaction are often taken for granted by traditional approaches to development and standard economic theory. Contracts and property rights are assumed to be in place, and what transpires in the informal economy is scarcely taken into account. In fact, most development initiatives tend to focus on the official economy, the formal legal system, and institutions at the national rather than the local level.

However, most poor people do not live under the shelter of the law, but far from the law's protection and the opportunities it affords. Informal local norms and institutions govern their lives and livelihoods, and where they are not excluded from the legal system, they are often oppressed by it. Because the poor lack recognised rights, they are vulnerable to abuse

by authorities that discriminate, seek bribes, or take the side of powerful interests who may wish to prevent the poor from competing economically or seek to evict them from their land. Such discrimination has massive consequences. The Commission finds that at least four billion people are excluded from the rule of law. It is the minority of the world's people who can take advantage of legal norms and regulations. The majority of humanity is on the outside looking in, unable to count on the law's protection and unable to enter national, let alone global markets.

Legal Empowerment of the Poor as a Development Strategy

When the law works for everyone, it defines and enforces the rights and obligations of all. This allows people to interact with one another in an atmosphere that is certain and predictable. Thus, the rule of law is not a mere adornment to development; it is a vital source of progress. It creates an environment in which the full spectrum of human creativity can flourish, and prosperity can be built. The Commission understands legal empowerment to be a process of systemic change through which the poor

and excluded become able to use the law, the legal system, and legal services to protect and advance their rights and interests as citizens and economic actors.

The law is the platform on which rest the vital institutions of society. No modern market economy can function without law, and to be legitimate, power itself must submit to the law. A thriving and inclusive market can provide the fiscal space that allows national governments to better fulfil their own responsibilities. The relationship between society, the state and the market is symbiotic. For example, the market not only reflects basic freedoms such as association and movement, but also generates resources to provide, uphold, and enforce the full array of human rights. It is processes such as these, in which the poor realise their rights and reap the benefits of new opportunities, which enable the fruition of citizenship – in short, legal empowerment.

If law is a barrier to the poor who wish to better their condition, if it is seen as an obstacle to dignity and security, then the idea of law as a legitimate institution will soon be renounced. If the law is accepted and understood as offering protection and equality of opportunity, and ensuring access to fair and neutral process, then the law will be revered as a foundation of justice.

There are no technical fixes for development. For states to guarantee their citizens' right to protection, systems can, and have to be changed, and changed systemically. Legal empowerment is a central force in such a reform process. It involves states delivering on their duty to respect, protect, and fulfil human rights, and the poor realising more and more of their rights, and reaping the opportunities that flow from them, through their own efforts as well as through those of their supporters, wider networks, and governments. The elements of legal empowerment are grounded in the spirit and letter of international human rights law, and particularly in Article 1 of the Universal Declaration of Human Rights, which declares, 'All human beings are born free and equal in dignity and rights.'

Democracy: Indispensable Means, Just End

The Declaration's fine words, written 60 years ago, are universally accepted but rarely fulfilled. If the poor are to be legally empowered, they must have effective, legally protected rights. These include the right to vote, the right to free expression, and the right to due process. It is a central purpose of democratic societies to provide these rights, and an ongoing challenge to do so consistently and equitably. International organisations, both regional and global, can help support the construction of democratic institutions through a variety of means.

Some have cautioned against democratisation while the rule of law remains imperfect. The Commission disagrees. Democracy and legal empowerment are kindred spirits, and are better synchronised than sequenced. In the absence of empowerment, societies lose the benefits that come from the free flow of information, open debate, and new ideas. Meanwhile, governments are not held accountable for unwise policies. There is a reason that no democracy has experienced famine, and that trends over several decades suggest democracies are less likely to become embroiled in conflict. There is, of course, no single model of democracy, but the needs of the poor can often be better voiced when decision-making is decentralised to the local level. The core principle underlying democracy, in all its forms, is that legitimate power is derived from the freely expressed will of the people. Strengthening democracy is essential to legal empowerment.

To the Reformers: Resistance and Reward

Transforming a society to include the poor requires comprehensive legal, political, social, and economic reforms. In the short term, reform is unlikely to seem an easy option. There is, however, a harvest to leadership. When the poor are able to find protection and opportunity in the legal system, practical benefits become evident. As the informal economy becomes documented the tax base is widened, increasing revenue for national development. Economic gains expand local markets and increase financial activity at all levels. As the rule of law spreads, the predatory networks that exploit vulnerable participants in the informal economy begin to unravel, and more and more people develop a stake in the reduction of crime and the maintenance of a peaceful social order. As this transformation occurs reform gains momentum and governments that have embraced reformist ideas are accorded increasing credibility, especially among political constituencies whose voices had previously gone unheard. In this way, legal empowerment can embody and live out a compelling narrative for progress.

Legal empowerment is not a substitute for other important development initiatives, such as investing more in education, public services, and infrastructure, enhancing participation in trade, and mitigating and adapting to climate change: instead, it complements such initiatives, multiplying their impact by creating the conditions for success. People living in abject poverty need immediate assistance and specially targeted interventions. The provision of quality education, especially for girls, could not be more urgent. The Commission is convinced that the world's four billion excluded possess significant capabilities. If states and laws are reformed to appropriately recognise the poor, if the law can be made to work for everyone, those who are excluded will quickly begin to transcend their current circumstances and contribute to the solution of otherwise chronic economic and social problems.

The Four Pillars of Legal Empowerment of the Poor

In the course of its deliberations, and on the basis of the work of its thematic working groups, the Commission developed a comprehensive agenda for legal empowerment encompassing four crucial pillars that must be central in national and international efforts to give the poor protection and opportunities. Legal empowerment can only be realised through systemic change aimed at unlocking the civic and economic potential of the poor. The Commission's agenda includes: *access to justice and the rule of law, property rights,* *labour rights, and 'business rights'.* * These four pillars reinforce and rely on each other. In their convergence and through their synergy, legal empowerment can be achieved.

First Pillar: Access to Justice and The Rule of Law

First among rights is that which guarantees all others: access to justice and the rule of law. Legal empowerment is impossible when, *de jure or de facto*, poor people are denied access to a well functioning justice system. Where just laws enshrine and enforce the rights and obligations of society, the benefits to all, especially the poor, are beyond measure. Ensuring equitable access to justice, though fundamental to progress, is hard to achieve. Even if the legal system is technically inclusive and fair, equal access to justice can only be realised with the commitment of the state and public institutions. Legal empowerment measures in this domain must:

- Ensure that everyone has the fundamental right to legal identity, and is registered at birth;
- Repeal or modify laws and regulations that are biased against the rights, interests, and livelihoods of poor people;
- Facilitate the creation of state and civil society organisations and coalitions, including paralegals who work in the interest of the excluded;
- Establish a legitimate state monopoly on the means of coercion, through, for example, effective and impartial policing;
- Make the formal judicial system, land administration systems, and relevant public institutions more accessible by recognising and integrating customary and informal legal procedures with which the poor are already familiar;

---

* 'Business rights' need not yet be regarded as a new term in law, but rather as derived from existing rights related to doing business of the individual, newly bundled together under this term on the basis of their vital instrumentality in the livelihoods of the poor.

Colombia © Jean-Luc Fievet 2007

- Encourage courts to give due consideration to the interests of the poor;
- Support mechanisms for alternative dispute resolution;
- Foster and institutionalise access to legal services so that the poor will know about laws and be able to take advantage of them;
- Support concrete measures for the legal empowerment of women, minorities, refugees and internally displaced persons, and indigenous peoples.

Second Pillar: Property Rights

Ownership of property, alone or in association with others, is a human right. A fully functioning property system is composed of four building blocks: a system of rules that defines the bundle of rights and obligations between people and assets reflecting the multiplicity and diversity of property systems around the world; a system of governance; a functioning market for the exchange of assets; and an instrument of social policy. Each of these components can be dysfunctional, operating against the poor. When the system fully functions, it becomes a vehicle for the inclusion of the poor in the formal economy, and a mechanism for their upward social mobility. When the entire system or a single component is dysfunctional, the poor are deprived of opportunity or discriminated against.

As reforms of property rights are inherently risky, full attention should be paid to securing the rights of the poor. Women, who constitute half the world's population, own only 10 percent of the world's property. Indigenous people and others also experience active discrimination. To ensure group rights, imaginative legal thinking is required. Providing the absolute poor with rights and access to assets means direct social interventions.

To be fully productive, assets need to be formally recognised by a system encompassing both individual and collective property rights. This includes recognition of customary rights. Embodying them in standard records, titles, and contracts, in accordance with the law, protects households and businesses. Evictions should only be an option in circumstances where physical safety of life and property is threatened, where contract agreements have been breached, or under fair eminent domain procedures. It must be by due legal process, equally applicable, contestable, and independent, and where the cost of eviction is fully compensated. Property rights, including tenure security, should not only be protected by law, but also by connecting the property of the poor to wide societal interest (by increasing the range of validation of their tenure security). The possibility is opened for the poor to use property as collateral for obtaining credit, such as a business loan or a mortgage. It encourages compliance by attaching owners to assets, assets to addresses, and addresses to enforcement; that is, making people accountable. As such, property reform can strengthen access to legal identity and to justice. Property records unify dispersed arrangements into a single legally compatible system. This integrates fragmented local markets, enabling businesses to seek out new opportunities outside their immediate vicinity, and putting them in the context of the law where they will be better protected by due process and association of cause. Legal empowerment measures in this domain must:

- Promote efficient governance of individual and collective property in order to integrate the extralegal economy into the formal economy and ensure it remains easily accessible to all citizens;
- Ensure that all property recognised in each nation is legally enforceable by law and that all owners have access to the same rights and standards;
- Create a functioning market for the exchange of assets that is accessible, transparent, and accountable;
- Broaden the availability of property rights, including tenure security, through social and other public policies, such as access to

housing, low interest loans, and the distribution of state land;
- Promote an inclusive property-rights system that will automatically recognise real and immoveable property bought by men as the co-property of their wives or common-law partners.

Third Pillar: Labour Rights

The poor may spend most of their waking hours at the workplace, barely surviving on what they take from it. But labour is not a commodity. In the same way that property and the physical assets of the poor are recognised, so must the greatest asset of the poor – their labour and human capital – be effectively recognised. The legitimacy, even the acceptability, of the economy depends upon basic labour rights, as does the development of human capital necessary for sustained growth. In turn, the continuous improvement of labour and social rights depends on a successfully functioning market economy. The typical and tired pattern of low productivity, low earnings, and high risks must be replaced by the fulfilment of the *Fundamental Principles and Rights at Work* and the *Decent Work Agenda*, and the strategy to provide protection and opportunity to workers in the informal economy, a coalition described as an emerging global social contract. Here is how:
- Respect, promote, and realise freedom of association so that the identity, voice, and representation of the working poor can be strengthened in the social and political dialogue about reform and its design;
- Improve the quality of labour regulation and the functioning of labour market institutions, thereby creating synergy between the protection and productivity of the poor;
- Ensure effective enforcement of a minimum package of labour rights for workers and enterprises in the informal economy that upholds and goes beyond the *Declaration of*

Indonesia UNICEF/HQ07-0690/Josh Estey

Fourth Pillar: Business Rights[2]

The Commission holds it to be self-evident that the poor are entitled to rights, not only when working for others but also in developing their own businesses. Access to basic financial services is indispensable for potential or emerging entrepreneurs. Just as important is access to protections and opportunities such as the ability to contract, to make deals, to raise investment capital through shares, bonds, or other means, to contain personal financial risk through asset shielding and limited liability, and to pass ownership from one generation to another.

Fundamental Principles and Rights at Work;

- Increase access to employment opportunities in the growing and more inclusive market economy;
- Expand social protection for poor workers in the event of economic shocks and structural changes;
- Promote measures that guarantee access to medical care, health insurance, and pensions;
- Ensure that legal empowerment drives gender equality, thus meeting the commitments under ILO standards that actively promote the elimination of discrimination and equality of opportunity for, and treatment of, women, who have emerged as a major force in poverty reduction in poor communities.

These rights may not be equally relevant to every entrepreneur but they are instrumental in poverty eradication and economic development. They must be accessible to all the many micro, small, and medium enterprises in the developing world — many operated by women - that employ a large portion of the labour force. The success or failure of this economic sector will often spell the difference between economic progress versus stagnation, increased employment versus widespread joblessness, and creation of a broader society of stakeholders versus deeper inequality leading to a weakened social contract. Legal empowerment measures in this domain must:

- Guarantee basic business rights; including the right to vend, to have a workspace, and to have access to necessary infrastructure and services (shelter, electricity, water, sanitation);

- Strengthen effective economic governance that makes it easy and affordable to set up and operate a business, to access markets, and to exit a business if necessary;
- Expand the definition of 'legal person' to include legal liability companies that allow owners to separate their business and personal assets, thus enabling prudent risk-taking;
- Promote inclusive financial services that offer entrepreneurs in the developing world what many of their counterparts elsewhere take for granted – savings, credit, insurance, pensions, and other tools for risk management;
- Expand access to new business opportunities through specialised programmes to familiarise entrepreneurs with new markets and help them comply with regulations and requirements, and that support backward and forward linkages between larger and smaller firms.

Institutional Momentum and Implementation

To succeed, legal empowerment has to lead to systemic change, including institutional reform. In a comprehensive agenda, rather than a piecemeal approach the four pillars of legal empowerment reinforce each other. Effective institutions and laws that spell out rights and obligations give individuals the confidence to cooperate with others over time and distance, thereby steadily creating wealth. Productivity gains released through reform in one area carry over into others. Mechanisms for social protection and labour rights are closely linked to the development of a competitive and productive business environment. In legal empowerment, good things go together.

Political leadership is imperative. A comprehensive agenda will be best run not by individual ministries, in competition for support and attention, but by presidents and prime ministers in cooperation with ministers of finance, justice, and labour. Using their political authority, presidents and prime ministers can drive the agenda forward and create vital political momentum. But high office is not a precondition to effective leadership. Citizens and grass-roots organisations can create valuable momentum for change by educating the public and rallying around the themes of legal empowerment. Many improvements in the lives of the poor have been realised through social innovation. Legal Empowerment must also travel bottom-up.

The Commission's recommended approach to legal empowerment is different from traditional approaches to legal and institutional reform and does not involve off-the-shelf blueprints for implementation. National and local contexts differ, creating a varied array of hurdles and opportunities for reform that must be taken into account. Success, however, is likely to share common features. Broad political coalitions, drawing leaders from across society and committed to championing policies, will smooth the way to legal empowerment and help overcome resistance, diversion, and delay. Knowledge of, and being attuned to, the political context and reforms based on a deep and shared understanding of local conditions in both the formal and informal economy is essential. The gender dimension needs critical attention in all four domains, as do indigenous peoples' rights and customary law. The poor are not the objects of legal empowerment, but its co-designers and facilitators. They must participate and provide feedback in all phases of the reform, including the close monitoring of the results. Reform must grow from the realities and the needs of the poor. The Commission is convinced that success is most likely where the will to achieve democracy is greatest.

How to Proceed in the Multilateral Realm

While the government is the key responsible actor, the 'duty bearer' in human rights terms, in a process of Legal Empowerment of the Poor, the United Nations and the broader multilateral system can help by lending their full support. The international non-governmental community can do the same. More specifically:

- The legal empowerment agenda must be integrated as a core concern of global multilateral agencies such as the World Bank, UNDP, ILO, FAO and UN-HABITAT. In their distinctive ways, these agencies influence how governments establish and implement the rules that define economic and social protections and opportunities. Their strategies and operational approaches must change in order for them to provide strong, sustained, and coordinated support to Legal Empowerment of the Poor. UNDP should take the lead and work with other UN agencies to develop a coherent multilateral agenda for legal empowerment;
- Legal Empowerment of the Poor must also become a core mission for regional political organisations, regional banks, and regional UN institutions. These organisations can work closely with national leaders both to assist governments engaged in reform and to exert a normative influence on governments less willing to embrace reform;
- Civil society and community-based organisations can contribute by connecting the poor to political institutions at every level, advocating better representation for the poor, organising support for reform agendas, and serving as independent auditors of the political system;
- The business community can smooth the way

for legal empowerment through the UN Global Compact, and by supporting and participating in reform efforts on a local and national basis;
- Religious communities and indigenous spiritual traditions can play a unique and vital part in translating the moral imperatives of legal empowerment into concrete action;
- Various professional associations, including jurists, lawyers, land administration officials, surveyors and urban planners, can also play a role in gathering and disseminating information in their respective communities and networks. They can offer political support for legal empowerment and access to justice reform, as well as increased funding for necessary legal aid and other services.

Together, these initiatives should give:
- Coherent support for legal empowerment efforts in individual countries;
- Foster a political consensus for legal empowerment at the regional and global levels;
- Create new instruments for supporting legal empowerment, such as:
  o A 'Global Legal Empowerment Compact' as a first step in codifying core rights and spelling out a framework for their realisation;
  o Mechanisms for tracking progress at every level;
  o A clearing-house for recording, storing, and disseminating experiences and lessons learned related to legal empowerment;
  o Public-private partnerships;
  o A global initiative to promote grass-roots knowledge and innovation.

In summary, the vast majority of the world's people live outside the law. This is a recipe for national and global stagnation. A state that is blind to itself is destined to fail. When so many people are excluded from the rule of law, societies are unable to reach their potential; every element of the economic system – from productivity and savings to investment and markets to planning and innovation – is deprived of energy and assets. This exclusion makes it harder for governments to meet national needs, and creates social conditions that can generate civil unrest and social disintegration.

The remedy for exclusion is inclusion through Legal Empowerment of the Poor. This is important economically, politically, socially, and morally. A country with laws and institutions that do not shut out the poor will benefit from the contributions of its entire population and from a legal, social, and economic order in which all segments of society have both a voice and a stake. Such countries will be better able to build national cohesion, and more likely to find a positive niche in the competitive world marketplace. The world as a whole will benefit as more and more states undertake the reforms needed to empower the poor. Such initiatives will help to reduce the pressures created by refugee migrations, under-development, famines, environmental neglect, health emergencies, and strife. In an interdependent world, we will all do better if our neighbours are both able to count on the protections of law and expected to live up to their responsibilities under it.

After all, our era is one of seismic shifts, not only in the economic order but also in the creation of a global public domain. Myriad ungoverned interactions flow between states, from the obvious to the near invisible, from the malign to the beneficent. Some must be curbed, some controlled, some eased and encouraged. Yet, as at the national level, our global institutions remain blind to much of reality, equipped rather for yesterday than today, hampering our attempts to grapple with each new problem we face. Who can deny that we all share a responsibility to protect: one

which we are far from meeting? Whether for climate change, trade, migration, or security, the world will expect fair rules for the 21st century, rules offering protection and opportunity for all in accordance with shared human rights obligations.

Time for a Renewed Anti-poverty Agenda

It is time for a renewed anti-poverty agenda aimed at including the vast majority of the world's population in the systems of rights and obligations that have shown their ability to foster prosperity over the past 60 years. It is the responsibility of national and global leaders, and of us all, to enlarge that circle of opportunity and extend the reach of protection – not by replicating the trajectory of rich countries but by finding means that enable every country to chart its own path. Though methods will vary, the goal is the same – to enable and empower the poor to succeed both as individuals and contributors to the economic and social well-being of their communities. Further inaction and delay will send human talent early and unused to its grave, and blight the lives that remain.

Making poverty history cannot be accomplished through legal empowerment alone, but it is hard to see how it can be done without it. Legal Empowerment of the Poor recognises the complexity of society and the rich potential of the poor. By unleashing their energy and creativity, we have it within our power to forge a better, more prosperous, equal, and humane world. The time has come to unite in support of that vital and transforming task.

The Commission observes
people, the majority of the
excluded from the rule

1
Making the Law Work
for Everyone

that around four billion
world's population, are
of law.

B efore the violence came, Margaret Atieno Okoth sold cabbage six days a week at a cramped stall in Nairobi's Toi market, alongside vendors hawking everything from second-hand shoes to bicycle parts. Her meagre earnings allowed her to send only three of her 12 children to school, while her husband, John, sought odd jobs in the middle-class estates within walking distance of their home. But no matter how hard Margaret worked, her family had to subsist in a one-room tin shack with no electricity, water, or sanitation. They were trapped in Kibera, a squalid slum where a million Kenyans struggle to survive and poverty is passed down from one generation to the next.

In thousands of such settlements around the world, poor people like Margaret have no legal identity – no birth certificate, no legal address, no rights to their shack or market stall. Without legal documents, their ability to make the most of their efforts and assets is limited, and they live in constant fear of being evicted by local officials or landlords. Criminals prey on them; corrupt officials fleece them. And, as witnessed in the recent violence in Kenya, security eludes them. Shortly before the violence erupted, Joseph Muturi, who ran a small clothing business in Toi market, told friends and colleagues: 'I know that in a matter of hours all this can disappear.' He was mainly concerned with the threat of bulldozers flattening the market to make way for more powerful economic interests. In the end, the violence was political, triggered by a disputed election. For thousands of people in Toi market, the event simply proved the fundamental truth of Joseph's words. Everything did disappear. There was no security and no protection when it was needed the most.

Such problems may seem intractable. But change *is* possible. Just visit Delhi's Sewa Nagar market.

'I'll never forget how terrible life was before,' says Mehboob, who sells plastic wares at Sewa Nagar. 'We struggled to survive through honest, hard work, but it was almost impossible. The police and local officials demanded bribes, threatening to evict me or confiscate my goods. I had to pay up, but I was still harassed and beaten up. My produce was seized and I lost count how many times I was evicted. I never thought things could be any different.'

A visitor to Sewa Nagar nowadays would scarcely recognise the awful conditions that Mehboob painfully recalls. The market throngs with shoppers rooting out bargains from the clean and well-maintained stalls that jostle for their attention. Madan Sal is selling dried fruit, Santosh tempts female clients with bangles and cosmetics, Raju does a brisk trade shaving the men – and none of them is afraid any more.

The source of this remarkable transformation is simple yet profound. Whereas previously Santosh and the other traders were not legally entitled to trade, now they have obtained official licenses to do so. On paper that may not seem revolutionary, but in practice it empowers the market's poor traders to make their hard work pay. In exchange for a reasonable monthly rent, the traders now have secure rights for their pitches. 'We no longer have to pay bribes,' explains Mehboob. 'I feel good because I'm earning honest money and paying my taxes.'

Most of India's street vendors are not as fortunate. The country's municipal laws prohibit street trading without a license, yet Delhi, with a population of over 15 million people, has issued fewer than 4,000. It is estimated that 99 percent of the country's 10 million street vendors are forced to work illegally. Instead of being protected by the law, they are excluded from it.

Part of the problem is that the voices of the poor are not heard. Sewa Nagar's transformation came about because a Delhi-based action group called Manushi led a grassroots campaign to lobby government officials for change. That won the backing of the local authority and members of parliament, at least in public.

'We have been facing a great deal of violence and threats in recent months,' says Madhu Kishwar of Manushi. 'But the good news is that Manushi has received strong support for this work at the highest levels, cutting across party lines.'

'The Prime Minister's office has intervened in the matter and given instructions that this project should not be disturbed. The lieutenant governor is also supportive, as is the deputy commissioner of the area. But local politicians are after our blood and the local police are playing a dubious role for obvious reasons. This had become a bribe-free zone – something the lower-level police cannot stomach. They are also under heavy pressure from politicians who are desperate to keep vending spots under their control, not only because this yields a lot of income but also because they can then armtwist these people to come for political rallies, do election work for them, and be available whenever they need to have a show of strength.'

For Madhu, the battle is only just beginning. 'This pilot project is part of a much larger campaign that seeks to free the lives of the self-employed poor in India from needless bureaucratic controls and extortionist mafias,' she says. 'It recognises that poor people's enterprise plays a vital role in the country's economy and that they have a right to earn a living free from harassment, extortion, beatings, and other human-rights abuses.'

Sewa Nagar's metamorphosis demonstrates a basic, but often overlooked, truth: law-induced exclusion and poverty go hand in hand, yet neither is inevitable. If Sewa Nagar can change, so could Kibera. Margaret could yet enjoy a better life too. Even after disaster, new beginnings are possible.

The Importance of the Law

Far from being a luxury that the poor can live without, effective legal rights are a necessity for everyone. Poor people's exclusion from the law is not just desperately unfair, it denies them an opportunity to improve their lives and it stunts the development of poor countries.

Around half the people in urban areas worldwide live in squatter settlements and work in shadow economies. An even larger absolute number of the poor are in isolated rural areas with limited secure access to land and other resources. They operate not within the law, but outside it: they enter into informal labour contracts, run unregistered businesses, and often occupy land to which they have no formal rights. In the Philippines, 65 percent of homes and businesses are unregistered, in Tanzania 90 percent. In many other countries the figure is over 80 percent. In terms of GDP, the informal economy accounts for over a third – and rising – of the developing world's economy.[3]

When would-be entrepreneurs set out to legally register a business, bureaucratic red tape and costly fees thwart them. A recent Inter-American Development Bank study of 12 Latin American countries found that only eight percent of all enterprises are legally registered, and that nearly 23 million businesses operate informally. The owners of these businesses cannot get formal bank loans,[4] nor can they enforce contracts or expand beyond a personal network of familiar customers and partners. An estimated two billion people are without access to basic financial services.[5] As a result, the poor have no choice but to accept insecurity and instability as a way of life.

The exclusion of the poor from the law is a crucial issue, yet it has received little practical attention – until now.

This report by the Commission on Legal Empowerment of the Poor is the first to highlight how giving the world's poor women and men access to justice, and underpinning and enabling property, labour, and business[6] rights – the legal rights that most people in rich countries take for granted – can empower them to change their lives for the better.

The Commission brings together illustrious women and men of different backgrounds, varying political persuasions, and a wide range of expertise. We have spent the past three years sifting through a mountain of evidence, observing the plight of the poor first hand, and seeking out the views of a variety of people all over the world – policymakers and ordinary citizens, rich and poor, business people, civil society and community-based organisations, international development experts, and representatives of slum dwellers. We have listened and we have learned. This report reflects many voices, but above all those of the poor. The message that comes through loud and clear is that the world has not grasped the importance of making the

THE COMMISSION ON LEGAL EMPOWERMENT OF THE POOR

The Commission on Legal Empowerment of the Poor is the first global initiative to focus on the link between exclusion, poverty, and the law. Launched by a group of developing and developed countries including Canada, Denmark, Egypt, Finland, Guatemala, Norway, Sweden, South Africa, Tanzania, and the United Kingdom, it has been hosted by the United Nations Development Programme (UNDP) in New York.

Co-chaired by former U.S. Secretary of State, Madeleine Albright, and the Peruvian economist, Hernando de Soto, it brought together eminent policymakers and practitioners from around the world. The full list of Commission members is at the opening of this report.

Legal empowerment is not about aid, but about helping poor people lift themselves out of poverty by working for policy and institutional reforms that expand their legal opportunities and protections.

law work for everyone to provide protection and opportunity. And the consequence of this reflects the continuing truth in Rousseau's words, 'Man is born free but is everywhere in chains.'

Progress and Frustration

The world economy becomes ever more dichotomous. Recent decades have witnessed unprecedented advances in economic growth and human development. In much of the world, living standards have improved, as have life expectancy, infant survival, access to clean water, schooling rates, and the treatment of women. Some 500 million people have escaped extreme poverty in the past 25 years.[7]

This remarkable progress has gone hand in hand with an evolution in development-policy thinking and practice. We have learned important lessons about what works and what does not. What began in the 1950s, as a narrow agenda of investing in infrastructure to spur economic growth, is now much broader. It encompasses measures to boost social development and meet the basic needs of poor people. It covers macroeconomic reform and the encouragement of private-sector-led growth. It considers issues such as trade, debt, environment, and gender. And, since the early 1990s, it proposes democratic governance and a vibrant civil society.

At the turn of the 21st century, the United Nations' Millennium Summit adopted the Millennium Declaration and set eight ambitious Millennium Development Goals (MDGs). These goals mark an unprecedented global commitment to reducing poverty and promoting human development: better food security and healthcare, improved access to education, less discrimination, and greater environmental sustainability.

Extreme poverty has fallen. And yet, eradicating global poverty remains an elusive target. Sub-Saharan Africa is not on-target for a single Millennium Development Goal.[8] Around the world, inequality is on the rise. Market solutions and macroeconomic rigour have not delivered all they promised. And, although efforts towards more sustainable development and democratic governance are clearly important, they have failed to deliver the breakthroughs that many had hoped for.

Flaws in the international system continue to undermine development efforts. The inchoate state of international law and its application leaves international security, let alone international justice, a chimera. Even though international trade is vital for developing countries, the Doha Development Agenda negotiations at the World Trade Organisation are

Zimbabwe © UNICEF/HQ02-0344/Giacomo Pirozzi

stalled. There has been progress on debt relief, but much remains to be done. Most donor countries still fall far short of their internationally agreed commitments to give 0.7 percent of their gross national income in aid. Overseas aid is not always targeted at alleviating poverty, and is often delivered in a poorly coordinated and ineffective way.[9]

The insidious effect of the law's failings on the lives of the poor has long been a theme of great commentators – Charles Dickens, for example, in almost all his novels. Among economists, Douglass North was one of the first to note that the policy prescriptions associated with traditional economic theory failed to capture the nuances and complexities of informal

economic activity. North and later economists such as Nicholas Stern shifted their focus from standard theories of how markets operate, to the importance of market institutions such as property systems, the business environment, and labour.[10] These institutions, they argued, shape ordinary people's economic activity and are highly resistant to change because of entrenched interests

From this new understanding of the challenges associated with economic development came a focus on better governance of these critical market institutions. Particular emphasis was put on the investment climate and the rules and norms affecting property and labour. Stern and others also advocated for the creation of mechanisms to enable poor men and women to participate in decision-making that affects their lives. They called for greater investment in people, through education, improved access to information, and capacity development in key public institutions.[11]

Stern's focus on poor people's assets and capabilities, and the functioning institutions needed to release their potential, mirrors Amartya Sen's emphasis on the freedom of the poor to shape their own lives. Sen identifies political and economic governance – and the quality of relevant institutions – as intrinsic and instrumental to the expansion of human development as freedom. This encompasses access to, and the quality of, education and health, as well as political and market participation. Sen's agenda of development as freedom is virtually synonymous with the political, social, and economic empowerment of people grounded in human rights. Development thus understood is both a moral imperative and, according to Sen, the route towards prosperity and poverty reduction.

Based on the lessons of the past 50 years, the OECD's Development Cooperation Directorate has set out guidelines for increasing the effectiveness of aid and development cooperation, and they are similarly comprehensive: ensure local and national ownership of the development process; promote good governance, including democracy, human rights, and the rule of law; turn from traditional development projects towards more policy-based approaches and direct budgetary support; and encourage the active participation of civil society.[12]

'The poor' is shorthand for a huge variety of people who have low incomes and struggle with problems such as hunger, ill health, and inadequate housing. They live in remote rural villages, as well as in urban shantytowns. They work as household service providers, subsistence farmers, casual labourers, street vendors, and trash recyclers. Many are from under-represented ethnic minorities – often internal or international migrants who have moved to an area where they lack clear legal status. Many have been displaced by war and civil unrest. Others are indigenous peoples who have been excluded by the dominant society. The poor are disproportionately women.

But if this approaches a comprehensive sense of what is required, the challenge of how to get there is a journey only just begun. Support of the rule of law is a case in point: it has had its own ebb and flow in the last 50 years, but a growing body of literature paints its practice as incipient.[13] Old-school approaches to Law and Development require revision.

Many factors are neglected altogether. Most development initiatives still tend to focus on the official economy, the formal legal system, and other established institutions, and are implemented mostly at a national rather than a local level. For instance, programmes promoting access to justice and the rule of law generally emphasise formal institutions such as parliaments, the electoral system, the judiciary, and the executive branches of government. Economic assistance tends to focus on improving the investment climate for registered or foreign businesses.

Yet most people in developing countries, particularly the poor, scarcely interact with national institutions and the formal legal system. Their lives are mostly shaped by informal local norms and institutions, such as the conditions of the slum in which they live or the degree of corruption of local officials. Big national reforms pass them by.

Addressing the Four Billion Poor and Excluded

In *The Bottom Billion*, Paul Collier argues that the international community should focus its aid efforts on the world's very poorest countries, which have a combined population of a billion or so, and are often in, or recently emerged

at effective poverty reduction and economic recovery. But focusing only on the bottom billion is a flawed and insufficient response to global poverty. Collier argues we should 'narrow the target and broaden the instruments.' This report is an essential part of the broadening, but no narrowing should accompany its application.

We know there are depressing figures for the number of people living on less than one dollar a day (those in extreme poverty)[14] and those living on less than two dollars a day (those in moderate poverty).[15] But the Commission observes that around four billion people, the majority of the world's population, are excluded from the rule of law.[16] At best they live with very modest, unprotected assets that cannot be leveraged in the market due to cumulative mechanisms of exclusion. The legal empowerment agenda speaks to all these four billion. Their poverty in income terms may vary but their right to equal protection and opportunity under the rule of law does not.

'Ending extreme poverty is crucial not solely as a matter of compassion. The world economy will benefit enormously from the contributions of those who are able to move from a state of dependency to full participation. (…) The Commission's mandate is daunting but also vital, for legal empowerment can add much to the world's arsenal in its ongoing struggle to save and enrich human lives.'

Madeleine Albright

Four billion people are not protected adequately by law and by open and functioning institutions, and, for a range of reasons, are unable to use the law effectively to improve their livelihoods. Yet these four billion are not a monolithic group. Those in extreme poverty are typically asset-poor and will not be able to get out of poverty merely by legal reforms. Their situation can only be improved through a range of measures, from protection of their livelihoods to access to additional resources and services, and systemic reforms to make public institutions accessible and fair. Those living in moderate poverty have some assets and income, which can enable them to take advantage of institutional change.

from, conflict. Collier argues that aid is most needed, and can potentially do most good, in such countries. But he believes that aid will do relatively little to boost development and reduce poverty in other developing countries, which have other resources to tap, such as trade, foreign direct investment, and taxation.

International development assistance is indeed essential for the poorest countries and for societies recovering from conflict. Donors should prioritise these countries and target funding

For all these people, protection of their assets is fundamental. But protection of what they have is not enough, for they are poor and their possessions meagre. They deserve a chance to make their business operations, no matter how small or even micro they are, more productive, and they are entitled to decent working conditions. Reforms of the institutions they relate to are essential for their empowerment. Only through such systemic change will the poorest be able to take advantage of new opportunities and be attracted to joining the formal economy.

But we must also address those that, while not in extreme or moderate poverty, are nevertheless not able to use the law to their advantage and are in constant danger of joining the ranks of the very poor. The legal empowerment agenda seeks to prevent this slippage and strengthen the poor with more capacity and resources. Empowerment of this group may also have an additional positive development impact for both economic and political reasons. The economic reason is that the empowered poor in this stratum stimulate market interactions. In many countries it would strengthen the chain of value addition among the poor and the lower middle class, and ultimately the higher strata. Politically, strengthening the hand of these poor can gain more voice, and capacity for self-organisation and, ultimately, for self-empowerment. While legal empowerment of this broader range of poor people may not – thankfully – consume a large part of scarce aid resources, it is a critical component for effective poverty reduction and socio-economic development. Legal empowerment is a versatile agenda for all the four billion excluded.

Realising Rights through Political Change

Legal empowerment is anchored in the basic principles of human rights articulated in the Universal Declaration of Human Rights – and the subsequent global and regional international human rights conventions – beginning with Article 1: 'All human beings are born free and equal in dignity and rights.' The implications of this simple statement could not be more profound. Indeed, out of familiar and established principles, comes a radical agenda of legal empowerment, not a technical fix, but an agenda for fundamental reform. All citizens should enjoy effective protection of their basic rights, assets and livelihoods, upheld by law. They should be protected from injustice, whether caused by their fellow citizens or government officials, all of whom – high and low – must be bound by the law. The international community has a duty to support legal empowerment both as an expression of these principles and as a core strategy for achieving the Millennium Development Goals.

This is intimately related to democracy, the ultimate bottom-up process; at once the indispensable means to, and the expression of, numerous human rights, and the least worst way mankind has devised for arranging its affairs. Legal empowerment can lay the ground for successful democratisation, yet it need not delay it – the two need to work in tandem. In much of the world, including the old democracies, the development of democracy is stalled, and the search for innovation and renewal must be redoubled. Where democratic practice can flourish, so will legal empowerment, and individuals and their communities. It is an advantage in practice and principle that legal empowerment is less prescriptive to development than other approaches, having as its aim the increased capacity of the poor, including in the public sphere, so that decisions on the nature of development are theirs, rather than being pronounced from reports such as this.

Legal Empowerment is the Way Forward

The Commission believes poverty can be eliminated, but only with a radical shift in thinking and approach by governments and international institutions. Some argue that ending poverty depends largely on unleashing market forces while others favour greater reliance on the guiding hand of government. But both of these traditional views are missing a vital part of the picture. Development depends on more than markets and economic policy; it also depends on how laws and institutions function and relate to citizens. That, in turn, reflects how power and influence are distributed in society. The problem for Sewa Nagar market was not an absence of enterprise or a lack of government regulation; it was the lack of a politically agreed and supported legal underpinning.

We believe it is time to go beyond the outdated battle lines of yesteryear; left versus right, state

'Public servants often believe they are helping the poor as a favour. They feel totally distant from the poor and often do not want to engage with them.'

National Consultation in Uganda

versus market, local versus global. Our agenda is not based on abstract theories or utopian pieties; it reflects the realities of poverty and exclusion experienced by poor people themselves. It focuses on removing the barriers that hold the poor back, and building a framework of laws and institutions that provide genuine protection and opportunity for all. The tools needed to act are available and ought to have broad political appal.

The Commission believes that poverty is manmade, a consequence of our actions and our inaction. By design or by default, markets, laws, institutions, and politics often fail to serve the common good, excluding or discriminating against poor women and men. Democracy is often more of a mantra than a reality; the rule of law, in practice, is often rule by law, arbitrarily and unequally applied. While people in poor countries may have rights on paper, that is often where they remain. Frequently the only laws that people know are informal rules, some traditional, others more recent.

In most rich countries, in contrast, the majority of people have effective rights and duties, whether as workers, business people, tenants, or property owners. If their rights are violated, they have recourse to the law; if they breach their obligations, legal action can be taken against them. The knowledge that legal rights and obligations can be enforced, if necessary, guides people's everyday actions, and this certainty allows them to pursue economic and other opportunities. In effect, the prosperity of rich countries is created through a variety of sophisticated instruments and norms such as limited-liability companies, partnerships and cooperatives, tradable assets, labour contracts, venture capital, insurance and intellectual property – all of which rely on an effective framework of law and functioning institutions. Even the most developed countries, however, are far from eradicating exclusion and legal disempowerment. There may be great problems in affording representation, or no legal framework to create a micro-credit bank,[17] and migrants may languish on the outside of society, surrounded by a world they cannot access. Legal Empowerment of the Poor is not an agenda any part of the world can regard with complacency.

Empowering poor people to realise their

enormous potential would allow them to grasp their destiny both as citizens and as pioneers of development. That, in turn, would enable countries to be better equipped to face some of the challenges of globalisation – among them trade competitiveness, full employment, environmental sustainability, and access to technologies. All of this is not a substitute for other important initiatives, such as investing more in social services and infrastructure, enhancing participation in world trade, and making efforts to mitigate and adapt to climate change; it complements them. Legal empowerment provides 21st-century solutions to the age-old problem of poverty and is a crucial component in addressing the new challenges of our time.

Making Poverty History

Making poverty history will be difficult. It demands popular pressure, political leadership at all levels, time, and huge efforts from poor women and men themselves. Yet the poor can only escape poverty if they are empowered to help themselves.

The stakes could not be higher. Our evershrinking world, torn between rich and poor, is not just desperately unfair; it is dangerously unstable. Our lives are inescapably intertwined; we can harm, or we can help each other. Thus globalisation not only poses a challenge; it also offers a choice. Act now and build a better world for all; or do nothing and put at risk everything we cherish.

That is why we must transform security and opportunity from the privilege of the few to the reality of all. Justice demands it, and so does development. Our core message is simple: making the law work for everyone offers protection and opportunity for all. This report details how, setting out the pillars of legal empowerment, its political and economic advantages, an agenda for reform, policy measures, phases and tactics, and action required at the international level.

The best practices of inform
building blocks for an
and a legitimate and incl

2

The Four Pillars of
Legal Empowerment

ality can provide the
attractive formal economy
usive legal order.

Like Margaret and John in Kibera, most of the world's poor live outside the ambit of the law, their penury both a cause and a consequence of their lack of effective legal rights. They struggle to survive, let alone better themselves, living in fear and insecurity, their efforts hindered at every turn. Because the system works against them, the poor have to run just to stand still.

They cope by devising their own solutions. They come up with 'informal' ways of doing things that blend customary practice with modern ingenuity (as do the rich, but for advantage not necessity). These sometimes very sophisticated informal structures guide how the poor live, work, and do business, obtain essential services such as education, water and energy, and protect and police their communities. For instance, the poor create informal means of adjudicating property, documenting transactions, guaranteeing and obtaining credit, creating business associations, dividing labour, and verifying identity.

While the poor often resort to informal means because they are, in effect, excluded from the formal economy, they sometimes choose to operate informally because formal institutions are dysfunctional or corrupt. Formality and informality often overlap and interact – many workers and businesses decide how much to engage with state institutions by weighing the benefits of doing so against the potential costs of not doing so.[18] Indeed, the distinction between the formal and the informal economies is often blurred: a broad spectrum of arrangements of varying degrees of formality and informality exists.

'The lives of each and every person living in the formal city are served directly or indirectly by thousands of informal workers who work long hours, often under terrible conditions, for incomes that hardly cover their food costs. They also live with the constant threat of eviction from their informal settlements.'

Sheela Patel

But informal institutions can leave the poor vulnerable to corruption, exploitation, bureaucratic meddling, the strong arm of the law, and criminals. The justice meted out can be exemplary (developed countries could learn much from some ancient systems of restorative justice), but equally it is often brutal and discriminatory, not least against women. Economic transactions remain unpredictable, insecure, and limited. The limited reach of local networks circumscribes opportunity – tapping national or international markets is almost impossible. Informality is therefore unlikely to be a springboard for development. It provides few opportunities for economic growth and limited revenue for public investment in essential services – such as health, education, infrastructure and justice – that would benefit the poor.

However, the objective of legal empowerment is not to 'fix' the informal economy. That would be the equivalent of treating symptoms rather than causes, and punishing efforts to cope rather than supporting them. The principal cause of widespread informality is the failure of formal laws, institutions, and governance. Consequently, many people shy away from the state and public institutions and remain in the traditional, informal economy. Myriad local informal practices and solutions help sustain these communities. But if the best practices of informality could provide the building blocks for

an attractive formal economy, and a legitimate and inclusive legal order, the horizons of the poor would be greatly expanded. The core part of the legal empowerment agenda is therefore not only to incorporate these building blocks into the formal legal system, but also to reform the existing *formal* institutions to make *them* open, accessible, and legitimate.

The Concept of Legal Empowerment

Legal empowerment is the process through which the poor become protected and are enabled to use the law to advance their rights and their interests, vis-à-vis the state and in the market. It involves the poor realising their full rights, and reaping the opportunities that flow from that, through public support and their own efforts as well as the efforts of their supporters and wider networks. Legal empowerment is a country and context-based approach that takes place at both the national and local levels.

The Commission's approach to the concept of legal empowerment is depicted in the diagram above. Two key conditions for Legal Empowerment of the Poor are identity and voice. The poor need (proof of) a recognised identity that corresponds to their civic and economic agency as citizens, asset holders, workers, and businessmen/women. Without a voice for poor people, a legal empowerment process cannot exist. Crucially this voice needs to be based on information and education on the one hand, and organization and representation on the other.

Starting from the livelihoods of the poor, composed of their assets and their activities,

The Concept of Legal Empowerment

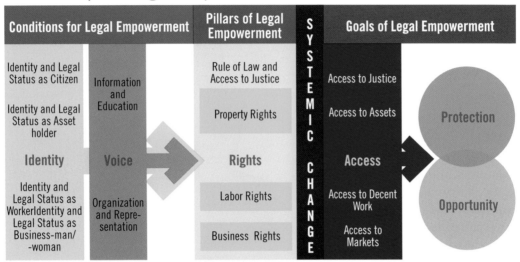

Conditions for Legal Empowerment		Pillars of Legal Empowerment	S Y S T E M I C C H A N G E	Goals of Legal Empowerment	
Identity and Legal Status as Citizen	Information and Education	Rule of Law and Access to Justice		Access to Justice	Protection
Identity and Legal Status as Asset holder		Property Rights		Access to Assets	
Identity	**Voice**	**Rights**		**Access**	
Identity and Legal Status as WorkerIdentity and Legal Status as Business-man/-woman	Organization and Repre-sentation	Labor Rights		Access to Decent Work	Opportunity
		Business Rights		Access to Markets	

three empowerment domains are identified as vital: property rights, labour rights and 'business rights.'[19] Access to justice and the rule of law are to be considered the fundamental and enabling framework that supports realization of these rights. The core bundle of rights cannot be fully effective unless there is a realistic option of enforcing them. Legal empowerment is thus a comprehensive framework with four pillars, access to justice and the rule of law, property rights, labour rights, and business rights.

As a reform process, legal empowerment requires parallel and coordinated interventions. The whole process is to be understood as iterative and the relationship between the legal empowerment process and systemic change is mutually reinforcing. Poor people who are legally empowered will have increased voice and identity; they will have more influence on institutional and legal reforms and social policies, which, in turn, will improve the realisation of their rights as citizens, asset holders,

workers, and business people. Legal Empowerment of the Poor requires systemic change, but if the poor are truly empowered this fundamentally improves the relationship between the state and all its citizens. With identity in their different roles, a voice in the processes of change, and improved rights in the three

> 'The most tangible face of the state to the poor is the police officer in the favelas who often engages in behaviour that violates their fundamental rights.'
>
> National Consultation in Brazil

empowerment domains, the poor will effectively have increased access to justice and the rule of law, improved access to assets, more access to decent work, and better access to markets.

Women, indigenous peoples, and vulnerable groups must be fully and fairly included in all phases of the legal-empowerment process. For them 'equal' access may not be enough; active promotion and facilitation of these groups' meaningful participation may also be necessary to ensure just outcomes and their full participation in the process.

The end goals of legal empowerment are expanding protection and opportunity for all: protecting poor people from injustice – such as wrongful eviction, expropriation, extortion, and exploitation – and offering them equal opportunity to access local, national, and international markets.

Identity and voice as key conditions of legal empowerment

Afghanistan © UNICEF/HQ07-1168/Shehzad Noorani

'Everyone has the right to be recognised before the law' is one of the most central human rights. The state is thus under the obligation to give formal, legal recognition that a person exists. Legal empowerment requires an affordable document with which the bearer can prove his or her identity. Without such proof of their legal identity the poor, in particular, are often excluded from the formal protections of the state legal system and as beneficiaries of public goods and services.

People also need information about their rights and how they can help shape decision-making. They need a say in how their society and the economy are organised. Voice requires education, which, like information and identity, is too often asymmetrically available to the rich and poor. And the poor need representative organisations of their own choosing. There is strength and protection in numbers. Organisations can demand and negotiate reforms and engage with the state more broadly. Almost all poor people have access to groups or associations of some

'Legal empowerment is also about opportunity: the poor can and do generate income, and are incredibly resourceful and ingenious in scratching out a living. In cities and villages around the developing world, they sell goods and services in the streets and organise markets that governments refuse to recognise.'   Kumi Naidoo

kind – small farmers' cooperatives, trade unions, small business associations, community-based organisations, women's associations, or faith-based communities – that can provide a more effective platform from which to advance their rights.

Human Rights

Legal empowerment finds its normative basis in globally agreed standards of human rights and should always meet or exceed these global standards. Human rights should guide the legal empowerment process, in particular institutional and legal reforms, as well as social policies that aim to reconfigure the relationship between state and citizens at the national and local level.

Property rights are human rights

The *Universal Declaration of Human Rights* stipulates that 'everyone has the right to own property alone as well as in association with others' and that 'no one shall be arbitrarily deprived of his property.'[20] According to the *European Convention for the Protection of Human Rights and Fundamental Freedoms*, 'every natural or legal person is entitled to the peaceful enjoyment of his possessions. No one shall be deprived of his [or her] possessions except in the public interest and subject to the conditions provided for by law and by the general principles of international law.'[21] The *American Convention on Human Rights* holds that 'everyone has the right to the use and enjoyment of his property. The law may subordinate such use and enjoyment to the interest of society.' It further provides that 'no one shall be

deprived of his property except upon payment of just compensation, for reasons of public utility or social interest, and in the cases and according to the forms established by law.'[22]

'A discussion of human rights quickly brings to mind the atrocities taking place in Darfur, or Congolese warlords drafting children into their ranks, or migrant women and children sold into sexual slavery. (...) But while these crises call the world's attention to some of the most visible and dramatic examples of human injustice, the lack of basic human rights endured by millions living in absolute poverty, originates in the underlying structures of many societies, which systemically divide rich from poor, powerful from powerless. In fact, more than half the world's population lives outside recognised and enforceable laws, without effective legal means to protect their families, homes or other possessions.'

Mary Robinson
English translation of editorial in Madrid's El Pais of June 1, 2007

The same legal intention is expressed in the *African [Banjul] Charter on Human and Peoples' Rights*, which holds that 'the right to property shall be guaranteed. It may only be encroached upon in the interest of public need or in the general interest of the community and in accordance with the provisions of appropriate laws.'[23] In the context of peace–building, and in dealing with the complex situation of refugees and internally displaced persons (IDPs), property restitution is considered an important human rights issue. According to representative texts of the international community, there is no just peace without the institution of private property and without the restitution of arbi-

29

Turkey © UNICEF/HQ05-1217/Roger LeMoyne

trarily expropriated property or an equivalent compensation for expropriated goods.[24] *The Convention on the Elimination of All Forms of Discrimination against Women* states in Article 16, 'States Parties shall take all appropriate measures to eliminate discrimination against women in all matters relating to marriage and family relations and in particular shall ensure, on a basis of equality of men and women: (h) The same rights for both spouses in respect of the ownership, acquisition, management, administration, and enjoyment and disposition of property, whether free of charge or for a valuable consideration.'

Labour rights are human rights

An important part of international human rights law encompasses fundamental labour rights such as freedom of association and protection of the right to form and join trade unions; elimination of forced or compulsory labour in all its forms; just and favourable conditions of work; elimination of discrimination in access to employment, training and working conditions; equal pay for men and women for work of equal

value; and abolition of child labour, stipulating a minimum age for admission to employment.

Business rights as a new area of human rights?

Business rights need not yet be regarded as a new term in law. Rather it is a composite of existing rights of individuals and groups of people to engage in economic activity and market transactions. The Commission has bundled these rights together on the basis of their vital instrumentality in the livelihoods and economic prospects of the poor. Business rights include the right of people to start a legally recognised business without arbitrarily applied regulations or discrimination in the application of norms and procedures. It focuses on removing unnecessary barriers that limit economic opportunities, and on protecting the investments that people make in their enterprises, however small they may be. Business rights derive from political and civil rights as well as economic and social ones. The right to organise and the freedom of association, for instance, underpin the right to form business cooperatives, other companies and employers' and workers' associations. Business activities are an expression of an entire class of liberties, namely freedom of association, freedom of movement, freedom to develop one's own talents, and freedom to exchange legitimately acquired goods and services.

The rationale for promoting business rights is their connection to fundamental freedoms of the individual, as well as the immense importance of small- and medium-sized enterprises in overcoming poverty. A large proportion of the poor work in such businesses (even more so if we include farming). As such enterprises grow, they provide increased labour and rising incomes. Even modest growth in income at this level makes a profound difference to security and quality of life. The more inclusive the formal market becomes the better the opportunities for expanding the coverage and quality of labour rights, which in turn builds human capital.

A human rights agenda

We propose an ambitious agenda for change and an effective strategy for implementing it, all of which will have to be negotiated and agreed locally and nationally. At the same time, we strongly urge the international community to expand the basis of legal empowerment in international human rights law. The core rights of legal empowerment deserve to be further developed in regional or global legal empowerment compacts and eventually in international human rights treaties.

Such a framework can buttress national reform, but in order for reforms to benefit the poor they must be built from the bottom-up, not top-down or outside-in. Participation and ownership by the poor themselves is key to any success. The Elders-led campaign, Every Human Has Rights, is a good example of how

the human rights agenda can be embedded in culture and civil society, a step towards legal empowerment.[25] Reforms that are imposed, no matter how well intended, rarely take root in society. To be recognised as relevant and legitimate by a broad majority of people, laws must be anchored in existing values, customs, and structures, and also be consistent with international human-rights obligations. This is especially true for legal empowerment, which is about giving voice to the poor and teeth to their rights. It is an advantage in practice and principle that legal empowerment is less prescriptive than other approaches to development, having as its aim the increased capacity of the poor, including in the public sphere, such that decisions on the nature of development are theirs, rather than being pronounced from reports such as this.

The Four Pillars of Legal Empowerment and the Scale of the Problem

Access to justice and the rule of law as the fundamental and enabling framework is the first pillar of legal empowerment. The three other pillars are the domains of empowerment derived from the livelihoods of the poor: property rights, labour rights, and business rights. In each pillar the scale of the problem that the Commission is trying to address is surveyed, before turning to solutions in the chapters ahead.

First pillar: Access to justice and the rule of Law

Access to justice and the rule of law are central to legal empowerment. Reforming the law on paper is not enough to change how the poor experience it day to day. Even the best laws are mere paper tigers if poor people cannot use the justice system to give them teeth. Even the best regulations do not help the poor if the institutions enforcing them are ineffective, corrupt, or captured by elites. It is therefore vitally important to reform public institutions and remove the legal and administrative barriers that prevent the poor from securing their rights and interests.

Legal identity is a cornerstone for access to justice. Despite the unequivocal provision in the Universal Declaration of Human Rights, tens of millions of people lack a formally documented legal identity. It is estimated that more than seven in ten children in the world's least-developed countries do not have birth certificates or other registration documents.[26] This prevents many of them from accessing education and healthcare. It leaves them more vulnerable to exploitation, such as child labour and human trafficking. And, without documentary proof of their existence, their parents may find it hard to interact politically, economically, and even socially outside their local communities. Absence of legal documents may be used to block them from taking advantage of anti-poverty programmes specifically intended for them.

Even when in possession of a legal identity, most poor people still experience lack of access to justice. State institutions tend to serve the established networks of the political and economic elites rather than the poor. Comparative global statistics on access to justice are hard to come by; even accurate measurement is tricky.[27] A country that is thronging with lawyers, for instance, may not necessarily have a better and fairer legal system. But figures can still indicate the scale of the problem. In India, for example, where there are reportedly only 11 judges for every million people, more than

20 million legal cases are pending, and some civil cases take over 20 years to reach court.[28] Around a million cases are pending in Kenya, over 300,000 before the High Court in Nairobi alone.[29] The average judge in the Philippines has a backlog of 1,479 cases.[30]

'The justice system is characterised by delays in the dispensation of justice, lack of institutional capacity and inefficient systems of law enforcement and congestion. These problems exist mainly because of a shortage of adequately trained personnel and a lack of essential equipment and facilities at both federal and regional levels.'

National Consultation in Ethiopia

Laws that are vital to the poor are often unclear, contradictory, outdated, or discriminatory in their impact. In the Philippines, for instance, settlers must prove they lived on land before 1992 in order to obtain formal rights; informal settlers can rarely demonstrate such proof, while settlers since 1992 are excluded by the law altogether.

The existence of effective procedural rights – functioning mechanisms to implement rights – is also important. A recent study of five countries in Central America shows that poorly designed or missing procedural laws are an important reason for ineffective substantive law. This may partly explain why constitutional rights remain on paper only, taxes are not collected, and public investment in social services stays below 'guaranteed' leves.

The poor may be unable to access the justice system because they do not understand it, or lack knowledge about it. They may be illiterate, which severely hampers their ability to interact with the justice system. In many countries, the law is drafted and administered only in the national language, which many poor people may be unable to speak or read. In almost all African countries, for example, the justice system operates solely in English, French, or Portuguese, thereby excluding the majority of the population that speak only local languages. Courts may be far away, under-funded, and take years to decide cases. Bringing a case to court swiftly may require bribes. Judicial procedures may be inaccessible for those who lack legal representation, which

The most serious problems that the poor report in surveys of their legal needs surround changes in the major relationships that govern their lives and their assets. For example, since poor people usually live in family homes that have not been formally documented and registered, the death of the head of the family throws into question who owns it and who has a right to live there. In addition, land is often prepared for farming and then used without formal rights ever being established. The absence of formal rights leaves the poor vulnerable to eviction if the legal landowner changes, and makes due process and full compensation less likely during attempts at eviction by the public authorities. Similarly if her rights have not been for-malised, a woman who helps build a business with her husband is likely to lose everything in case of divorce. When communities jointly own pastures, share water, and use the same fishing grounds, it is almost impossible for people who move out to realise their assets, which effectively limits their freedom to change their way of life. At the same time new arrivals may be denied access to collec-tively held resources.

'Besides the fact that justice does not use a language that is easily understood, particularly by the poor, the illiteracy of the large majority of the Beninese constitutes a serious obstacle to their access to justice. It is often a source of incomprehension and suspicion: the poor may feel that justice is biased towards the rich, many decisions are rigged, and that judges are corruptible. The unfamiliarity towards justice translates into feelings of incomprehension, frustration, and disaffection.'

National Consultation in Benin

is generally too expensive for the poor. Restric-tions on who may practice law and provide legal services are other barriers that can block more accessible forms of legal services such as legal clinics and paralegals.

Difficulties in obtaining access to justice reinforce poverty and exclusion. As surveys of legal needs, crime, and victims demonstrate, the poor need better legal protection. Their personal security is often threatened. Many live in constant fear of eviction and expropriation.

Malign dependency is a high risk. Partners are tied to each other by specific invest-ments, which they risk losing if they leave the relationship. The poorest person in the relation-ship generally has most to lose – tenants and employees tend to have more invested in a specific piece of land or business than a landlord or employer has invested in them. Women often devote more time and effort to their family and its assets than their husbands do, which makes it difficult for them to escape an unhappy marriage and vulnerable to exploitation.

Despite their need for the legal system, many poor people steer clear of it, and from state institutions in general. They believe, often correctly, that these institutions will not help solve their problems. Even if the system could conceivably provide adequate redress, it may take too long, cost too much, and require expertise that they lack.

The principle of equality before the law is fundamentally important, yet incredibly difficult to fulfil. Even fully-fledged democracies with well-functioning state institutions struggle to do so. In countries where democracy is weak, institutions are more likely to be captured by elites. All too often, the law is a tool of the state and ruling elites to use as they please – an option for the few, not an obligation that applies equally to all.

Haiti UNICEF/HQ94-0806/ NICOLE TOUTOUNJI

Second pillar: Property rights

The relevance of property rights goes way beyond their role as economic assets. Secure and accessible property rights provide a sense of identity, dignity, and belonging. They create reliable ties of rights and obligations within a community, and a system of mutual recognition of rights and responsibilities beyond it. For many poor individuals and communities, land is more than just an aggregate of occupied and used plots. It is the expression of a way of life, which they should have the opportunity to improve by their own efforts.

Starting out as ownership over parcels of nature, property arrangements have evolved enormously to cover land, other concrete assets, and ever-expanding abstractions such as pollution quotas, financial products, inventions, and ideas. Overwhelming evidence, from all over the world, shows that functional property relationships are associated with stable growth and social contracts, whereas dysfunctional property relationships are associated with poor, unequal, and unstable societies. When property rights are out of peoples' reach, or rights are subject to competing claims, their assets are often not secure and their economic potential remains severely inhibited.

Yet most of the world's poor lack effective property rights – they are without secure tenure, unaware of their legal rights, or unable to exercise them. This is true not only in the poorest states, but also in more prosperous ones such as Brazil, China, and Russia. The intrinsic economic power of their property remains untapped, and the poor unable, for example, to provide collateral on a loan to increase their incomes or improve their businesses. Insecurity hits the poor hard. They can be subject to arbitrary evictions, forced off their land at any time without compensation, and are powerless in disputes over assets with powerful actors. Their livelihoods are under constant threat, and there is little to encourage future investment in their land or small-scale business. In many countries, state institutions do not provide the protection the poor need and are entitled to.

Analysis of the World Bank's Country Performance and Institutional Assessments (CPIA) shows the extent of the problem. Based on a rating of 1 (lowest) to 6 (highest), only five of the 76 developing countries surveyed in 2005 had property rights and rule-based governance rated 4 or above – and all five were small island states.[31] This means that the property rights of most people in developing countries are not protected, that contracts are not enforced, and that registries and other institutions required to protect property, function poorly or not at all.[32]

The assets of the poor may be documented through informal local arrangements that provide some protection and liquidity. But these are rarely recognised by national institutions and do not allow capital to be leveraged more widely. Whatever their economic assets, people have the right to remain underemployed. Owners cannot use their assets to get loans, enforce contracts, or expand beyond a personal network of familiar customers and partners. Their property is often vulnerable to seizure through force or law. Moreover, informal capital is invisible and unproductive for the national economy. And, since the poor are unable to participate in the economy beyond their immediate vicinity, possibilities for trade are diminished.

This is a huge wasted opportunity. In Peru, for instance, informal capital is estimated at US$74 billion. The figure for Haiti is over US$5.4 billion; Honduras, nearly US$13 billion; Albania, nearly US$16 billion; Tanzania, over US$29 billion; the Philippines, over US$132 billion; Egypt, over US$248 billion; and Mexico, over US$310 billion.[33] That this informal capital cannot be put to its full use is particularly galling because it is already where it is needed most – in the hands of

Women are half the world's population, produce 60 to 80 percent of the food in developing countries, and are increasingly responsible for rural households, yet they own less than 10 percent of the world's property. Much of the misery in the developing world is due to statutory and customary property systems that disenfranchise women. Women often face barriers to owning, using, and transferring or inheriting property. Women face forcible eviction from their homes and their land (land over which they had customary or other rights) by family members, traditional authorities, and/or neighbours.   Sources: UN 1980; FAO 1999 Women's Right to Land and Natural Resources: some implications for a human-rights based approach.

poor people and their communities. External sources of capital, such as official aid and foreign investment, are less abundant and do not always reach the poor.

Uncertainty over legal ownership of forests, pastures, swamplands, and sources of fresh water – access to which most of the rural poor depend on for their livelihoods – is another huge concern. Already, nearly a third of the world's population suffers from a moderate to high water shortage. The World Commission on Water estimates that rising populations and economic growth will boost demand for water by half in the next 30 years, and some four billion people will be severely short of water by 2025.[34] The value of land and real property often depends directly on the existence of adequate water rights. In this situation, property rights will play a key role in defining who has access to water.

Vulnerable groups suffer most from a lack of property rights. Indigenous peoples are frequently victims of property discrimination; collectively held indigenous lands have often been declared public or unoccupied lands (and collectivity can be retained in formalising property rights). Women, who constitute half of the world's population, own very little of the world's property – as little as two percent in some countries. Rarely do they own more than 15 percent of it.[35] Even when women do have legal property rights, their actual control of land may be tenuous, since men often mediate access.

Third pillar: Labour rights

A well-designed system of labour rights should provide both protection and opportunity. The Universal Declaration of Human Rights sets out a series of labour rights, as does a long tradition of internationally agreed labour standards. Laws must protect vulnerable workers from exploitation without diminishing their opportunities for formal employment (excessive or inefficient regulations can do more harm than good). Our

After being cleared to eradicate the tsetse fly and create cropland and space for its growing population, the Shinyanga region became the Desert of Tanzania. In 1986, a governmental initiative known as the Hashi project empowered the agro-pastoralist Sukuma people, who used their ecological knowledge and strong traditional institutions to restore the productivity of their land. They re-established protected enclosures known as 'ngitili'. It did not take long for nature to respond. With the re-growth of acacia and miombo trees, shrub grass and herb varieties, came the return of birds and mammal species and of course cattle – a liquid asset within this rural community. Other lands became the property of individual families. Hard work and modest investment restored soil fertility and drove agricultural productivity up. Households' incomes, diet, and security improved significantly. Meanwhile, income from the shared enclosures have increasingly helped the communities pay for public services such as enhanced education, health service, and access to markets for their products. Hashi provides proof that empowerment, poverty reduction, and environmental sustainability go hand in hand

Source: The Wealth of the Poor World Resources 2005

outlook must switch from viewing labour as a raw resource to be extracted, to viewing labour as deriving from human beings who must become the subject of investment if prosperity is to be built.

Most of the world's poor scrape by doing insecure and poorly paid jobs in the informal economy. They are street vendors, rubbish collectors, construction workers, small-scale furniture makers, garment workers working from home, fishers, small farmers, and forest gatherers. Nearly all of the almost 500 million working poor earning less than one dollar a day, labour in the unofficial economy. Informal work accounts for over half of total employment in developing countries, and as much as 90 percent in some South Asian and African countries.[36] Roughly half of all informal workers are self-employed, often in disguised wage relationships; informal enterprises or households employ another quarter; and the final quarter is employed informally by formal businesses.

However hard they work, these self-employed workers, casual day labourers, and industrial outworkers cannot escape poverty. They have basic rights and protections in theory, but not in practice. They do not benefit from labour laws and collectiv-bargaining arrangements, because their employment relationship is unclear. They suffer inferior working conditions and job insecurity. They are typically denied access to state or employer benefits and social security.[37] Recognition and enforcement of the rights of individual workers and of their organisations is critical for breaking the cycle of poverty.[38]

Informal employment often expands in upturns as well as downturns. While recession throws people into informal work to survive, recovery may also boost informal employment in entrepreneurial small firms and sub-contracted and outsourced activities linked to the global production system.[39]

Women are particularly likely to work in the informal economy. In developing countries, excluding North Africa, over three in five women in non-agricultural work are informally employed. In countries where they are allowed to work, women account for anything from 30 percent to 90 percent of street vendors and 35 percent to 80 percent of home-based workers.[40] Over four-fifths of home-based industrial outworkers in the developing world are women. Moreover, women predominate in the lowest categories of informal work and typically earn less than men.

The last two decades have seen a marked increase in women's participation in the labour force. The pervasive segmentation of labour markets by gender suggests that women's labour did not simply substitute for men's. Rather, a parallel process has created low-paid and poor informal employment opportunities, primarily for women.[41]

Indigenous peoples have also often been forced into informal work by the loss of their traditional lands, relocation without compensation and basic support services, under-investment in education and health, and ill-adapted educational systems and materials.

More broadly, increasing global competition, labour regulations that are ineffective, outdated, or poorly designed, and rising informality, when taken together, widen the gap between labour law and the reality of the workplace.

Fourth pillar: Business rights

Most of the world's poor entrepreneurs operate informally and as a consequence an impressive share of the economy in developing countries is informal.[42] Ensuring their rights to vend, and to have a workspace and related infrastructure and services (shelter, electricity, water, sanitation), thereby facilitating the success of small and medium enterprises, would be an invaluable step towards poverty reduction. The poor occupy land that they do not hold title to, work in small, unregistered businesses, and rely on family and friends for loans or risk sharing. They are particularly vulnerable to the vagaries, corruption, and violence of criminals and officials. They have few means of settling disputes apart from bribery or violece.

Most Mexican citizens do not have access to banking and only 13 percent hold mortgage debt. In the absence of financial institutions, the poor and lower middle classes rely on pawnshops. The annualised interest rate they charge ranges from 48 percent in non-profit pawnshops to 160 percent in for-profit ones. Source: La Crónica de Hoy, 9 October 2006.

The economic opportunities of the poor are limited. They have difficulty accessing finance and markets, and can rarely obtain tax breaks and other business incentives. They must work around urban zoning regulations that prevent them from trading. They are often denied the right to use common and public resources. And they may be constrained by burdensome public health and sanitation rules, notably in the production of street food. As things stand, the four billion excluded have no prospect of obtaining the legal tools developed countries have used to create wealth. Most likely they will not be able to create a legal identity, obtain limited liability, associate with other entrepreneurs to integrate capital, access financial mechanisms to obtain liquidity, extend credit, contract with

'Utility connections (water, electricity and telephone) require a legally recognised property title or lease as a form of security. Thus, informal traders are often deprived of these services.'

National Consultation in Sri Lanka

employees, suppliers and customers, access export opportunities, and much more.

When the laws regulating small businesses are unfairly drafted, implemented, or enforced, or are simply too weak and inefficient, they leave the poor little option but to trade in the informal economy. Obtaining a license, the first step to registering a business, is often prohibitively expensive and difficult. In Kenya, for example, over 1,000 licenses govern entrepreneurial entry; over 130 separate laws regulate agriculture alone. Costly and cumbersome regulations prevent poor people from bettering themselves through enterprise, and stifle the economy's development.

The scale of the problem

The problem that the Commission addresses is of massive proportions. In each of the four pillars the problems are deep and affect poor people around the globe. Four billion people are excluded from the rule of law. We repeat: *Four billion people are excluded from the rule of law.* This Commission has an agenda to change this situation and we believe that addressing the issue of legal empowerment is both smart politics as well as good economics.

Promoting Environmental Sustainability and Addressing Climate Change

Securing land and resource rights for the poor can combat poverty as well as environmental degradation. The poor depend more directly on their local environment for their day-to-day survival than the rich. They bear the immediate brunt when ecological resources and services collapse. Yet evidence from around the world shows that reversing environmental damage such as over-fishing, water pollution, land degradation, and deforestation is closely associated with ensuring that local people and communities have ownership or stewardship over the environmental resources they depend on.[43]

Consider Namibia. Legal reforms in 1996 created a framework for the community-based management of natural resources, giving Namibians who form conservation areas legal rights to manage wildlife reserves. These secure rights have enabled rural Namibians to reduce poaching, and caused wildlife numbers and ecosystems to rebound.

Poor Namibians have also gained new entrepreneurial opportunities based on eco-tourism and related activities. These businesses provide a new source of income and work as well as a broader sense of purpose and dignity. Namibia's experience shows that devolving secure legal rights to local people can promote conservation and economic development.[44]

Climate change is an even bigger challenge – and the poor are most at risk. As the Intergovernmental Panel on Climate Change makes clear, a big cut in greenhouse-gas emissions is required to stave off disastrous global consequences. But UNDP's 2007 Human Development Report (HDR) documents the extent to which the poor are already affected. Poor women and men are the most vulnerable because they are living in marginal environments: areas prone to drought and desertification, areas at high risk of flooding, countries and communities with little scope to prevent or manage *(cont.)*

disasters or adapt to environmental change. When disaster strikes, disputes about land and other property rights are particularly contentious and difficult, not least when people are displaced. The destruction, or lack, of a valid, recognised system of property titles can lead to conflict and halt recovery and reconstruction in their tracks. During the cyclone in Bangladesh in 2006, many farmers' lands simply disappeared under water, forcing them to move. Climate change is likely to trigger future refugee crises as certain areas become uninhabitable.

'There are more floods now and the riverbanks are being washed away faster. There's nowhere to go. My land is in the river. I have nothing now.' Intsar Husain, Antar Para, north-western Bangladesh, 2007 (in HDR 2007/2008)

Negotiations pursuant to the global Convention on Climate Change offer opportunities to address the growing vulnerability of the poor through increased international cooperation on adapting to climate change, as well as efforts to limit it. A global agreement would need to include clear commitments to step up financing to help people in poor countries adjust. Legal Empowerment of the Poor should be part and parcel of the discussion since, without access to legal tools and protections, poor people will remain exposed. Climate-proofing infrastructure and improving disaster preparedness are not enough.

We urge the UN to include the legal empowerment agenda as a core element in the strategies for adaptation in the post-2012 negotiations on climate change. The UN Framework Convention on Climate Change (FCCC) recognises the right of the poor countries to receive support in adaptation to climate change. Since 2006 there has been an agreement on a Nairobi Work Programme on Impacts, Vulnerability and Adaptation to Climate Change. Legal Empowerment of the Poor should be included in these negotiations as a basic element of adaptation strategies and policies.

In a world in which carbon emissions urgently need to be restricted, 'cap-and-trade' carbon markets will provide important incentives for emission reductions and the transition towards cleaner and more sustainable technologies. These incentives should also generate a greatly increased demand for carbon-offset projects, including from developing countries. But the potential for the poor to access and benefit from this carbon financing, notably for projects addressing sustainable land management, will surely depend in important ways on their legal empowerment.

Thanks to the Kyoto Protocol, billions of dollars have been generated for investments in more sustainable solutions in developing countries, such as renewable energy. Such mechanisms must be expanded so that they can finance much broader investments in climate-friendly poverty reduction. Combining innovations in environmental finance and pro-poor legal reforms could provide a new model of development finance capable of reaching poor communities much more directly than conventional assistance.

The rehabilitation of degraded forests, grasslands, and agricultural land is an important part of mitigating climate change. Such lands, which have the potential to sequester significant amounts of carbon from the atmosphere, are found in large parts of Sub-Saharan Africa and many other developing regions. Through efforts to increase soil productivity, water retention, and vegetative cover, these degraded lands can contribute to meeting global climate goals while helping poor and vulnerable communities. Such investments should therefore qualify for financing from the Clean Development Mechanism or other instruments associated with the growing carbon markets.

The Kyoto Protocol has offered very few opportunities for land-related carbon finance. The new round of negotiations, triggered by the Bali climate conference in December 2007, provides the opportunity to address this shortcoming. However, equally important are the many issues related to a lack of clear rights to the ownership and use of land and other natural resources. Poor farming communities' lack of secure land rights denies them access to the carbon market as well as other forms of finance and services.

Carbon finance could help address both climate change and rural poverty. It is a great opportunity for bringing sorely needed investment to poverty-stricken rural areas. But without effective land rights, it will not happen.[46]

Legal empowerment is
emancipating the poor; it al
and security for

3
Legal Empowerment
is Smart Politics and
Good Economics

not just a matter of
so offers greater prosperity
society as a whole.

I n most countries, rich and powerful elites dominate politics and the economic sphere. Public policy and its outcomes are shaped by their interests, rather than those of the poor majority struggling to make ends meet. These economic and political inequalities tend to be reinforced by inequitable and dysfunctional laws and institutions, and the inability of the poor to access justice. This is not just unfair; it is short sighted. It may enable the rich to stay at the top of the pile for now, but at a huge cost. It erodes the state's powers, stunts economic growth, and breeds instability. Corruption and rent seeking[47] are particularly costly. In the worst cases, failing states descend into conflict. But even in countries where matters have not deteriorated as far, unjust systems that undermine security and restrict opportunity ultimately harm not just the poor, but society as a whole, even the elites.

Legal Empowerment is Smart Politics

Where formal laws and institutions do not serve the needs of the poor, politics gravitates towards informal channels. When governments are unable or unwilling to deliver protection and opportunity for all, the formal system's legitimacy and relevance are eroded. A vicious circle develops, with the decay of legal institutions and the growth of makeshift informal arrangements feeding on each other. The state hollows out. Society fragments. In the worst cases, the economy stagnates. Unrest brews. The legitimacy and authority of political leaders is undermined. At best this results in a precarious state of arrested development, at worst, collapse.

Governance matters, and more often than not poorer countries have less effective governance. Their people get less justice from the courts

> 'Many people do not know what their human rights are and are unaware of the meaning of having a right.'
> National Consultation in Mozambique

and are more subject to crime, corruption, and government interference in their lives. Good governance – in the form of institutions that establish a predictable, impartial, and consistently enforced set of rules – is crucial for achieving a more just, a more prosperous, and a more sustainable society.

Legal Empowerment of the Poor does not have to be a zero-sum game, where some people will

> 'Combating corruption requires raising awareness of the destructive consequences of corruption, enhancing the role of governmental and non-governmental monitoring institutions, asserting the role of the media, and creating an independent and impartial judiciary.'
> National Consultation in Jordan

gain and others will lose. As we have pointed out, legal empowerment starts with identity and voice. A successful strategy to give all people such an identity makes it harder to exploit poor people, but it does not reduce the identity of anyone else. Voice and representation for the poor does not deny others the same. In legal empowerment reforms, however, it is critical that the voices of the poor are not diluted. When institutional reform enhances poor people's access to justice, society as a whole

> 'The poor continue to perceive the law as mainly for the rich, recognizing the undemocratic reality that the law is the expression of the ideology of the dominant elite.'
> National Consultation in Philippines

is better off. Functioning property rights will contribute to functioning markets for assets, which will improve the productivity of land and other assets, thus reaping economic dividends for the poor. Property rights are crucial legal tools for the poor and as such they can be an instrument for inclusion and improved equality, rather than one of further marginalisation.

Legal empowerment is not just a matter of emancipating the poor; it also offers greater prosperity and security for society as a whole. Legal empowerment bolsters the state's effectiveness and legitimacy, and thus that of its officials and representatives at all levels. Bold leaders that champion Legal Empowerment of the Poor will win support far and wide.

A Political Challenge with Rewards

Undeniably, though, reform is tough. Any leader – whether a president, a political party leader in parliament, the head of a civil society or community-based organisation, a village chief or a slum warden – who wants to take up this challenge faces several particular difficulties.

For a start, the poor generally mistrust state institutions and the legal system, and with good reason. It is those institutions, with the power to establish and uphold the rules governing economic activity, which often perpetuate economic inequality. They must be reformed to work in the interests of all. In a Soviet-era study of one East European country, 82 percent of informal

business owners said bribing officials was necessary in order to continue operating their businesses.[48] Experience has taught the poor to be wary of politicians promising reform. They need to see tangible results to be won over. Politicians need to show that the formal system is changing to cater to their needs. Sewa Nagar market shows that it can be done.

There is also a widespread perception that promoting property rights will further the interests of the elite few. This is not necessarily true. It all depends on how such reforms are implemented and whether the interests of the poor are consistently safeguarded from the outset. Implemented efficiently, a well-functioning and inclusive property rights system is as important, if not more so, for the poor.

Myriad conventional experts on legal and development issues peddling technical solutions for every possible problem must also be bypassed. Quick technical fixes may seem appealing, but unless reforms are based on local needs and conditions, and negotiated and implemented by

getting the poor on side, they will not be able to take root and make a real difference.

Perhaps most importantly, a majority of society has to be persuaded that building a more inclusive and effective legal order is feasible and ultimately desirable for everyone. Utopian proposals elicit cynicism, revolutionary ones fear and resistance. The poor need a voice, an organisation, and information; the rich and powerful need persuasion and reassurance. Politics cannot be wished away. Powerful actors must be co-opted, won over. National leadership and broad coalitions for change are vital.

Legal empowerment, however, does not require its political champions to be saints (although that could be useful) but only to recognise an enlightened self-interest. Significant political capital accrues to the reformer. As informal economic activity sees opportunities within the formal system, the tax base is widened. Extra economic activity that results from legal empowerment further increases public revenue. As more and more people develop a stake in the reduction of crime and the maintenance of peace, the political base of reform advocates is extended. Moreover, leadership requires a credible vision of the future. Legal empowerment draws upon powerful notions of freedom, fairness, and solidarity, and can, therefore, shape a compelling vision. People understand the language of inclusion, particularly if they suffer exclusion on a daily basis. And what better political legacy than to have made a lasting contribution to the development of one's country, to have given people a real opportunity to better their lives.

Brazil © Moisés Moraes

Institutionalised in laws and practices, legal empowerment is a legacy that endures.

An Essential Role for Democracy

The plight of the poor is often rooted in political systems in which citizens are denied a voice; government institutions have no obligation to answer to the people, and special interests exploit resources without fear of scrutiny. Democratic rule can encourage the development of policies and delivery of programmes that address people's demands. It provides incentives and safeguards that allow all citizens, even the poorest, to reward officials who act in the public interest and hold accountable those who fail to address their needs. Famously, no democracy has ever experienced a famine.

While non-democratic governments may be able to provide security and basic services, democratic ones are more likely to respond to people's needs in a way that is perceived to be legitimate. There is empirical evidence suggesting that democracies outperform autocracies in per capita GDP growth and other social welfare indicators.[49] There is also a strong association among developing countries between democracy and well-being (as captured by the Human Development Index).

'Legal and judicial systems are not accountable.'

National Consultation in Tanzania

The self-correcting mechanisms of democracy, derived through checks and balances imposed by the branches of government, also foster accountability, curtail the abuse of power, and promote responsiveness to the concerns of the majority of the electorate. There is no substitute for a truly inclusive, participatory, and deliberative process, where alternative viewpoints are considered and the interests of poor and marginalised citizens are taken into account. Nobody is as wise as everybody.

Almost invariably, the poor suffer most from a lack of voice, representation, and influence – even in open and competitive government systems. Lasting political exclusion hardens into resignation and fatalism vis-à-vis the formal institutions and decision-making processes of the state. Vigorous efforts are needed to help citizens to organise and participate effectively in influencing decisions that affect their lives, as well as to enable political parties and parliaments to better represent voters' needs. Overly centralised power is frequently a constraint on meaningful citizen participation. Decentralisation and legal empowerment can mutually reinforce each other, because a government that is close to the people is more likely to be a government by and for the people. But even in the most decentralised systems exclusion can occur, so well functioning accountability mechanisms need to be in place.

Many democracies are fragile. They have inherited endemic problems such as debt, disease, ethnic divisions, poverty, and corruption. In many countries, checks and balances on power remain weak. But while controversy surrounds whether democratisation facilitates the rule of law, there is no disagreement that progress made in establishing the rule of law facilitates democratisation.[50] It would be more accurate to say that democratisation and legal empowerment must be synchronised rather than sequenced: for they are kindred spirits that must not be allowed to fall out. Democracy can help drive legal empowerment too, and both are intrinsic and instrumental to development.

Legal Empowerment is Good Economics

For years Venancio Andrade eked out a meagre living selling pots and pans on the dusty streets of Lima, the Peruvian capital, and neighbouring towns. He eventually taught himself how to make aluminium kitchen supplies, and in 1985 he scraped together enough money to buy a parcel of land in a barren industrial park on the outskirts of Lima. His ownership of property qualified Andrade for bank loans that helped his cooking utensils company grow, and he now heads the business association of Villa El Salvador, a sprawling shantytown of 400,000 that sprang up on the edges of the industrial park. The 62-year-old Andrade has five full-time employees on his payroll, and during peak production periods employs as many as 30 people. By his own reckoning, it was the acquisition of formal property titles that made him and other small businessmen in Villa El Salvador viable clients in the eyes of prospective lenders. 'Credit has allowed me to meet rising demand for my products when I need to produce more,' explains Andrade.[51]

Mountains of research confirm that good institutions are vital to the long-term success of economies. Indeed, some claim that the security of property rights has been historically the biggest determinant of why some countries grew rich and others remained poor.[52] This does not imply that property rights are the silver bullet. Rather it is an often overlooked, key ingredient of a broader legal empowerment and development agenda that will allow countries to develop modern economies. Making institutions and rules work for the broader public good is at the heart of this agenda.

Effective and inclusive laws, enforced through well-func- tioning institutions, bring a host of economic benefits that are so fundamental that they are often forgotten. They make transac- tions easier and cheaper. They foster predictability, security, and trust. They make enforce- able long-term contracts between strangers possible. That, in turn, permits a greater specialisation and division of labour, economies of scale, long-distance trade, and essential financial functions such as credit and insurance. Such features mark the difference between a rudimentary economy with a simple pattern of produc- tion and exchange and a vastly more complex and productive developed economy. Well-designed and fairly implemented laws can also promote competi- tion, investment, and innovation. What matters is not so much regulation or deregulation *per se*, but the quality of laws, regulations, and institutions.

Equity – by which we mean equality of protec- tion and opportunity – requires that the poor have the necessary security and a fair chance to participate in the formal economy. But so does efficiency: if the poor are unable to make the most of their talents, growth suffers. Bright ideas and profitable investments go untapped, poverty becomes entrenched, people's potential is wasted, and economic growth slows.[53]

Following a strike by Bogotá's public-cleaning and waste-management service in the mid- 1990s, the local government asked rag pickers to help. Heeding the city's call, they disposed of more than 700 tonnes of waste daily. Spotting a business opportunity, they organized themselves into the *Asociacion de Recicladores de Bogotá (ARB)*, an association of 25 waste-pickers' co-ops. But when the contract to provide solid waste-management services was subsequently put out to competitive tender, government legislation and the terms of the tender barred them from competing for it. Helped by pro bono lawyers, ARB demanded a constitutional review of this unfair provision and a writ of protection of human rights. Colombia's Constitutional Court accepted their arguments and granted them affirmative action for their inclusion in competitive bidding processes connected to waste management. Source: Ruiz-Restrepo 2007

Legal empowerment can make a difference in development. But it is not a panacea. Sound macroeconomic conditions also matter, as does openness to trade and foreign investment. Investment in education, training, infrastruc- ture, and essential services is vital. Under- pinned by legal empowerment, all of these will promote broad-based growth and poverty reduction.

The benefits of access to justice and the rule of law

To reap the full benefits of allocating property rights, defining employment relationships, and legally registering enterprises, rights must be enforceable and functioning institutions must implement them. While measuring the economic value of access to justice is notoriously difficult, most studies find that the rule of law makes a significant contribution to growth and poverty reduction. Yet studies that focus narrowly on the impact of the rule of law on the security of foreign investment understate its true economic benefits. Such studies neglect the value to the poor of being able to obtain redress for grievances.[54] They omit the wider benefits of making all economic transactions and relationships predictable, transparent, and fair.

Access to justice and the rule of law also makes it easier to settle disputes. Determining the ownership of assets, such as land, mining rights, and water, is often difficult. Duties to perform services, and intangible assets such as client relationships, may be difficult to define. The relationships in which these assets accrue are often hard to regulate in a contract, and particularly so for the poor. Disputes inevitably arise, especially when relationships change. A court or neutral arbitrator can help defuse conflict, reduce abuse, and enable the poor

to obtain redress. While being able to enforce contracts fairly is hugely valuable, unchecked legalism can cause defensiveness and uncertainty. Defendants need to be protected against the threat of flimsy claims, which have huge costs that are, in effect, a form of extortion. A balance needs to be struck.

The benefits of property rights

Property rights is to be understood as a bundle of rights and obligations between people and assets, reflecting the multiplicity and diversity of property systems around the world. In all property rights systems, creating security and predictability is fundamental. Property systems are a central facet of state functionality and are important indicators of its effectiveness.

In economic terms, to be fully productive, assets need to be formally recognized by a legal property rights system. Embodying them in standard records, titles and contracts in accordance to the law, gives households and businesses secure tenure that protects them from involuntary removal. Evictions should only be possible in exceptional circumstances by means of due legal process, which must be equally applicable, contestable and independent, and where the cost of eviction is fully compensated, only in circumstances where physical safety of life and property is threatened, where contract agreements have not been fulfilled, and where fair eminent domain procedures are applicable.

The rights of indigenous peoples depend on, and interact with, a wide range of measures and policies, such as those covering land tenure; the protection of endangered species; health, food, and agriculture; water quality; access to, and exploitation of, natural resources; environmental management; soil conservation; and the protection of cultural heritage. Within this broader horizon, **intellectual-property rights** may help create or protect indigenous rights. One example illustrating the use of intellectual property rights relates to traditional medicines in the People's Republic of China, in respect of which several thousand patents have been granted in past years.

Source: WIPO 2005

Property rights, including tenure security, should not only be protected by law, but also by connecting the property of the poor to wide societal interests (by increasing the range of validation of the tenure security) such as opening the possibility of using them as collateral for obtaining credit, such as a business loan or a mortgage. Such systems encourage compliance by attaching owners and asset holders to assets, assets to addresses, and addresses to enforcement. As such, property reform, if implemented in the right way, can strengthen access to legal identity and to justice. Property records unify dispersed arrangements into a single legally compatible system. This can integrate fragmented local markets, enabling businesses to seek out new opportunities outside their immediate vicinity.

Without effective property rights, managed by functioning institutions, advanced economies would shrivel. Conversely, their introduction could permit developing ones to make a huge leap forward. Consider China. A colossal challenge of poverty and inequality remains, as well as a great and historic debate on the nature and extent of property reform, but China's experience proves beyond doubt the instrumentality of property rights in the creation of wealth. The de facto securitisation of property, after the economy started to be liberalised in the 1980s, has generated US$7.4 trillion in capital for the country's economic expansion. This dwarfs the US$611 billion of foreign direct investment and almost US$46 billion of overseas aid that it has received.[55]

Evidence abounds that secure property rights boost business investment. Surveys in Poland, Romania, Russia, Slovakia, and Ukraine reveal that business people who believe that their property rights are secure reinvest as much as 40 percent more of their income than those who do not.

Farmers plough more back into their land too. In Ghana and Nicaragua, it was found that farmers with secure tenure invest more in their land.[56] Rural land in Brazil, Indonesia, the Philippines, and Thailand shot up in value by between 43 percent and 81 percent after it was titled. Rising land values reflect increased investment and feed into higher productivity, output, and incomes. In China, the combined effect of titling and price liberalisation increased farm production by 42 percent between 1978 and 1984.[57] Thai farmers who receive title to their land produce a quarter more than those who do not.

The value of urban land dramatically increased after it was titled – by 14 percent in Manila, by 25 percent in Guayaquil and Lima, and by 58 percent in Davao.[58] It also encourages people to do up their homes. A study of a shantytown in Argentina found that when squatters received legal title to their homes the number of houses with good quality walls rose by 40 percent, while those with good roofs increased by 47 percent.[59] Provision of secure rights over land in Lima augmented spending on housing renovation by 68 percent.[60]

When people's rights over their land are insecure, they have to devote valuable resources to physically protect it and often get tied down in conflicts over plot boundaries. A study of Peru found that nearly half (47%) of those without a property title had to hire watchmen to look after their plots. Families with more secure title were able to devote more time to finding better job opportunities. In total, household members spent 45 more hours a week in productive employment – the equivalent of adding an extra person's income to the household. Women who would otherwise have stayed home to protect it benefited most.[61]

Central African Republic / UN Photo

Protecting what existing assets they have is the first concern of the poor. Measures to achieve such protection will, in itself, empower poor people, secure their livelihoods, and make investments in their future more attractive. Property rights are fundamental to the life and operation of society and so their reform cannot be neglected. For this very same reason reform carries risks, thus special care must be taken to learn from past errors where benefits have been captured by local elites rather than the poor. Ensuring that property reforms do not weaken women's rights and communal rights of indigenous or pastoral groups is notoriously

Children stand to gain as well. Families in the Peruvian programme, for instance, are less likely to pack their young children off to work and more likely to send them to school. Since they have higher incomes from working longer hours outside their homes, they resort less to child labour.[62]

Empowering women with property rights makes a big dent in poverty and malnutrition. As women earn more, they tend to spend a bigger share of their income on keeping their children healthy and well fed. Ensuring women had effective property rights would thus underpin strong families and businesses.

difficult. The beneficiaries must be consulted, thus legal empowerment ensures that the poor participate in property rights systems voluntarily as they perceive the benefits exceeding the costs. It is a programme that grounds reform in the local realities and the needs and interests of the vulnerable.

Many indigenous lands have been, and still are, declared public or unoccupied lands because they are held collectively according to conceptions of ownership and access that do not fit well with imported property systems. This lack of status, recognition, and registration of collective user rights or group owned property, has huge consequences for indigenous asset holders and society at large. It is a critical issue for property rights reform globally. In addressing such issues in regions where the delimitation and identification of indigenous peoples is difficult and contested, it is better to focus on ensuring that indigenous land systems are recognised, standardised, and documented in accordance with the law. This sidesteps the troubled definition as to who is and who is not 'indigenous,' and has the added advantage of zeroing in on the systemic issues of indigenous or customary tenure regimes.

Customary tenure systems were once thought to provide insufficient security, but research shows that they can be flexible and responsive to changing economic circumstances.[63] In many developing countries, particularly in Sub-Saharan Africa, customary tenure systems represent an appropriate and cost effective way for the rural poor to secure access to land. A household, village, or kin group often provides insurance against risks, as well as access to informal credit and security. Customary systems are thus able to provide some of the essential economic functions of a formal property rights system. However, it is extremely important to ensure that the rights of women are safeguarded. Customary systems must pass the test of fundamental human rights obligations. Wherever assets can be represented in a standard form, the horizons of the economic activity of the poor will be correspondingly enlarged. When the local property system becomes documented and protected by law, it can be integrated into the national and international market economy, whatever its characteristics.

Whether through customary tenure, collective rights, or individual land titling, the poor need to be able to use their assets effectively. If they sell it to cope with a crisis, they might be worse off than before. The corollary areas of labour and business rights are critical for the poor to earn sufficient income through decent work and entrepreneurship in order to be able to leverage their property assets.

The benefits of labour rights

It is broadly accepted that labour is not a commodity.[64] The labour market is different from

> Removing children from work requires overcoming social prejudice, building enough good schools, and compensating poor families for the loss of a child's income. While these costs are not insignificant, the economic benefits of eliminating child labour – the greater productivity and earnings generated by more schooling and improved health – far exceed them.
>
> Source: UNDP IPC In Focus; Children in Poverty; March 2004

other markets in that it not only creates value it also shapes the distribution of income and prosperity. While progress requires that competition weed out failing businesses, people cannot be thrown on the scrap heap.

Ideological questions on regulation or deregulation have been debated endlessly. More important, however, is the question of how regulation can be used to promote decent work for the working poor. The focus should be on finding the right balance between security, supportive structures, and flexibility for firms in both the formal and informal economy, while working on reforms that will lower the costs of entry to the formal economy for small businesses so that labour rights can be more effectively enforced. Productive and decent work can raise individuals out of poverty.[65]

To promote decent work, it is necessary to eliminate the negative aspects of informality while at the same time ensuring that opportunities for livelihood and entrepreneurship are not destroyed, and promoting the protection of workers and economic units in the informal economy and their incorporation into the mainstream economy.[66]

Giving workers secure labour rights encourages them (and their employers) to invest in new skills that enhance their productivity. It would give them more bargaining power and consequently higher wages commensurate with their increased productivity. It would also enable them to obtain a fairer share of the profits of a business, protect them from exploitation, and ensure they have decent working conditions.

'Ugandans fear bankruptcy and the resulting loss of personal property.' National Consultation in Uganda

Secure workers are generally better motivated. They are more likely to invest in their future and that of their children. If they feel they have a stake in society, they will contribute more to it. So effective labour rights are not just about protecting workers; they also strengthen the economy and society.

While inadequate or inappropriate labour regulations can hinder productivity and access to decent work, deregulation can be counterproductive and leave workers vulnerable and insecure. Squaring the circle is not impossible – labour regulations should promote decent employment without discouraging businesses

from hiring workers legally. Legal empowerment can thus enhance productivity as well as decent working conditions.

The benefits of business righs

Legal registration can dramatically improve the productivity and profitability of informal businesses. Registration enables them to create hierarchies that permit the division and specialisation of labour. It helps them obtain fresh capital and accumulate the capital that they generate. It allows them to take on bigger risks, and thus to take advantage of new, potentially profitable opportunities. So while traditional and informal businesses certainly have their advantages, poor people should have the opportunity to legally register their businesses if they so wish.

Limited liability companies are among the most productivity enhancing legal institutions. They enable a business to constitute a legal entity distinct from its owners. This separates the personal finances of entrepreneurs from those of their businesses. If the business fails, the entrepreneur's family will not lose everything; if the entrepreneur falls on hard times, the business can still survive, or be sold. This encourages businessmen and women to take bigger risks, and thus earn higher returns.

Most informal businesses have to operate with no more than a limited amount of family capital. Entrepreneurs can sometimes borrow small sums from informal creditors, but only for short periods and at punitively high interest rates. These credit constraints prevent informal businesses from expanding, and expose them to greater financial and operational risks. Legally registered companies find it much easier to raise capital. Rather than relying on friends

Cambodia © Jean-Luc Fievet 2007

and family for finance, they can issue shares to a wider group of investors and borrow from micro-finance institutions, banks, and, eventually, capital markets. The cost of their capital is much lower, because they can tap a wider pool of finance, creditors have much greater certainty that they will be repaid, and investors can trade their shares more easily. When capital constraints are relaxed, new investments suddenly become possible. Entrepreneurs are able to diversify their risks, and opportunities that would have been missed can be seized.

Formal companies are also better able to commit to contracts and hold others to them. They do not need to dedicate as much time and resources to monitoring their agents and partners. They find

Public investment policies that promote the use of labour-intensive technologies have improved access to public procurement contracts for small local contractors in Andean countries. Activities range from micro-enterprises for routine road maintenance in rural areas to involving micro-enterprises in waste collection and street cleaning in urban areas. An ILO study shows, however, that access to public procurement for small local contractors is still very limited due to legal and institutional barriers. For example, countries may restrict contracts to enterprises recorded in the national contractor register or to recognized civil engineers or architects. Some regions have therefore introduced a 'small contractor card' and a register for local contractors, enabling small contractors to carry out small and medium-sized works in the local area, subject to certain minimum requirements.

Source: Yeng and Cartier van Dissel 2004. ILO

Making Trade Fair and Inclusive

World trade has soared in recent decades, delivering huge benefits for much of the world's population. But it could do far more to reduce poverty and improve opportunities for all. Open markets governed by predictable rules allow new entrants and start-ups a fairer deal thereby providing more opportunities, including for those who live in poverty but were previously locked out. A rules-based trading system internally and internationally is therefore a useful leveller and development tool.

Unfortunately, the WTO's Doha Development Round has stalled. The pressing issues of improved market access for developing countries and enhanced opportunities for the poorest countries have not progressed despite their laudable efforts to build trade-related capacity. In many countries, domestic economic policies have failed to stimulate job creation and growth with equity. For example, many countries rely on intensive natural-resource extraction to earn foreign exchange but have not combined this with policies to create new businesses and jobs around it. Opening markets must be complemented by appropriate change-management. Opening markets results in winners and losers, although accompanying measures that expand skills, infrastructure, and safety nets can help mitigate the negative effects. Hence trade-related policies are important drivers in promoting change and productivity.

Legal empowerment could play a role. Exclusion from property, business, and labour rights severely constrains opportunities for people and businesses to benefit from cross-border trade. In Mexico, for instance, only seven percent of businesses have the legal status and documents needed to trade with the United States and Canada under NAFTA. For Peru, only two percent are able to trade internationally. Expanding access to legal rights would give many more local businesses the opportunity to benefit from trade.

Registered businesses have greater access, not only to markets but also to the resources needed to grow and reap economies of scale, and thus become more competitive. Access to finance is important, but so too is access to risk sharing, information, and training. Most small farmers and industrial producers find it difficult to export. Their inability to penetrate foreign markets often reinforces gender inequalities, since women are disproportionately represented in these categories. They need property, business, and labour reforms to give them a chance to trade. They need innovative financial products and services and measures to protect informal workers through legally guaranteed and regulated employment and health insurance schemes.

it cheaper and easier to trade with strangers, even distant ones, and do not need to rely on relatives, close friends, and local contacts. New markets open up for them.

Formal companies are also more robust and adaptable. Since a company's capital consists of both tangible and intangible assets, such as good relationships with customers, its value is greater than the sum of its parts. If the owner of a formally registered business decides to leave, by selling its shares its value can be readily transferred. In an informal business, this is not possible. The firm's assets are the owner's personal property, as are its commercial

relationships. As a result, viable informal companies are often dissolved and their accumulated capital lost. For instance, when the owner of a legally registered company dies, the heirs inherit shares in the company. In the case of an informal business, the heirs inherit the physical assets of the business. Unsurprisingly, informal businesses often have very short lives, and much of their accumulated capital is lost.

Another weakness of informal businesses is that they do not usually have clear hierarchies and specialised roles. Because hiring workers is costly and contracts are impossible to enforce, most tasks tend to be concentrated in the hands of family or close friends. The family hierarchy often supplants the hierarchy of the business, and efficiency tends to suffer. Because legal companies can enforce contracts, they can hire strangers. This gives them access to a much bigger talent pool. Legal registration also allows companies to divide responsibilities among specialised workers organised through business hierarchies that make the most of their employees' talents. This greatly enhances productivity. Employees specialise in what they do best, while the costs of processing information, communication, coordinating productive activities, and acquiring and spreading knowledge are reduced.

Mexico © Maaike de Langen

The Benefits of Legal Empowerment of the Poor

Legal empowerment's benefits go wide and deep, unlocking human potential to startling results. This is a match for the scale of the problem. What's more, the Commission has a comprehensive agenda for change.

There are no technical fixes
    As national and local
    that the reform agenda
    and from the realities and

4
Agenda
for Change

for development.
contexts differ, it is critical
grows from local conditions
the needs of the poor.

The state has a duty to protect and the citizens have the right to protection. Thus, legal systems have to be changed, and this change must be systemic to establish a new balance between the authority of governments and the rights of citizens. The basic framework conditions of societies – national law, lawmaking, and law enforcement – have to be reformed.

This chapter sets out an agenda for change, with a series of reform measures for the four legal empowerment pillars. It draws from the work of the thematic working groups of the Commission, whose reports are published separately. It presents viable alternatives for government agencies, the private sector, civil society (including academia), and community-based organisations. A comprehensive reform agenda will have the greatest impact on poor people's

lives. However, as the situation in countries will differ, both with regard to national context and the challenges facing poor people, it is critical that the reform agenda grows from local conditions. There is no single right way forward. In some countries, certain policy measures are more urgent than others, and the timing and sequencing of reforms will vary. Every country and community needs to find its own way in the legal empowerment process. Poor people improve their lives incrementally; at each stage, an appropriate combination of legal empowerment reforms must be available to them.

An Agenda for Access to Justice

In order for the legal system to play a role in empowering poor people to escape poverty, laws that confer the appropriate mix of rights, powers, privileges, and immunities are needed – as are reforms in the public institutions and a

Reform Options

Justice
- Improved identity registration systems, without user fees.
- Effective, affordable and accessible systems of alternative dispute resolution.
- Legal simplification and standardization and legal literacy campaigns targeting the poor.
- Stronger legal aid systems and expanded legal service cadres with paralegals and law students.
- Structural reform enabling community-based groups to pool legal risks.

Property
- Institutionalize an efficient property rights governance system that systematically and massively brings the extralegal economy into the formal economy and that ensures that it remains easily accessible to all citizens.
- Promote an inclusive property rights system that will automatically recognize real and immoveable property bought by men as the co-property of their wives or common law partners, as well as clear inheritance rules.
- Create a functioning market for the exchange of assets that is transparent and accountable.
- Ensure that all property recognised in each nation is legally enforceable by law and that all owners have access to the same rights and standards.
- Reinforce property rights, including tenure security, through social and other public policies, such as access to housing, low interest loans, and the distribution of state land.
- Legal guidelines for forced relocation, including fair compensation.
- Recognition of a variety of land tenure, including customary rights, indigenous peoples' rights, group rights, certificates, etc., including their standardisation and integration of these practices into the legal system.
- State land audits with findings published to discourage illegal taking possession of public land.
- Simplified procedures to register and transfer land and property.

Labour
- Fundamental rights at work, especially freedom of association, collective bargaining and non-discrimination.
- Improved quality of labour regulation and its enforcement.
- Inclusive approaches to social protection, delinked from the employment relationship. Labour rights (health and safety, hours of work, minimum income) extended to workers in the informal economy.
- More opportunities for education, training and retraining.

Business
- Appropriate legal and regulatory frameworks, including enforceable commercial contracts, private property rights, use of public space.
- Fair commercial transactions between informal enterprises and formal firms. Financial, business development, and marketing services for informal enterprises.
- Micro business incentives, including government procurement, tax rebates, and subsidies. Social protection for informal entrepreneurs.

Former Yugoslavia (Federal Republic of) © UNICEF/HQ95-0848/Roger LeMoyne

porting outreach, and, if necessary, bundling registration services with other social services or traditional practices. It will also require creating incentives to register one's legal identity with the state by providing information, working through trustworthy local intermediaries, and minimising any adverse consequences of formal registration. The ultimate goal is not to increase registration rates, but rather to improve access to protections and opportunities. Though distribution of birth certificates alone will not lead to these goals, it is to be understood as an element of a larger reform agenda of legal empowerment.

legal and judicial system that can make these legal entitlements practically meaningful. As part of the access to justice effort it is necessary to audit all laws, regulations, procedures, and institutional set-ups. Laws that discriminate against the rights, interests, and livelihoods of the poor need critical evaluation and revision.

Ensure everyone has a legal identity

Legal identity is a cornerstone of access to justice. A legal identity for all people requires addressing a number of issues. These include lack of capacity in the identity registration systems of states, eliminating user fees associated with the system, sup-

Improve access to justice in the government bureaucracy

Many poor people rely on the bureaucratic system, be it related to land administration, urban planning, registration of assets and business, access to public credit schemes, etc.

'The law is not something that you invent in a university; the law is something that you discover. Poor people already have agreements among themselves, social contracts, and what you have to do is professionally standardize these contracts to create one legal system that everybody recognises and respects.'

Hernando de Soto

61

These systems may be open to abuse by those in power, serving the interests of the few, through corruption and lack of transparency, rather than acting as a framework for empowerment of the many. Hence, reform has to include both improved access to legal justice and improved access to justice in the government bureaucracy. Addressing the problems of the bureaucratic system may entail public administration reforms such as improving bureaucratic adjudication and grievance procedures, pursuing civil service reform to expand opportunities for performance incentives in government administration, and increasing decentralisation and redundancy in bureaucratic service provision. Administrative law reforms, including appropriately tailored expansions of freedom of information laws, impact statement requirements, and whistleblower protections, as well as appropriate but limited judicial review of administrative action, can also be important in increasing access to administrative justice.

and international bar associations and fostering an effective working relationship with the bar is important in developing targeted legal aid programmes that work. Bar associations could help gather and disseminate information in the legal community about access to justice issues, provide useful oversight, and offer political support for access to justice reform and increased funding for necessary legal aid services. They could also help determine the most worthy candidates for legal aid and

In Bangladesh, for instance, oral divorce is forbidden by the constitution but is still prevalent in poor rural communities A Bangladeshi NGO found that simply informing members of local customary courts that oral divorce was outlawed substantially reduced the practice. It was also possible to introduce norms from national law into community deliberations and mediation practices based on customary law and traditional norms.

Source: Golub 2000

Broaden the scope of legal services for the poor

Access to justice rests in great part on reasonable access to legal services. This can be achieved in several ways. One is gradually liberalising the market for legal services by reducing regulatory entry barriers – such as 'unauthorised practice of law' restrictions – for service providers, including non-lawyers, who are interested in offering legal services to the poor. Another is designing efficient legal aid systems, which may entail greater emphasis on legal assistance provided by paralegals[67] and law students, and the bundling of legal aid with other services.

Taking into consideration the role of national

possibly sponsor legal education programmes geared towards meeting the needs of the poor.

Related reforms include increasing the ability of poor people to secure financing for positive expected-value legal claims, and expanding opportunities for representative or aggregate legal claims such as class actions. The former requires appropriate liberalisation of the market for such financing, which may include expanding the opportunities for contingency fee arrangements, third-party investment in legal claims, and claim subrogation. While class actions have their flaws, situations in which large numbers of victims of the same or similar (often small) legal injury can pursue their claims collectively, do represent advantages in terms of affordability for the victims and hence in improving their access to justice.

Management of the courts

All people, the poor most of all, must have meaningful access to the courts to resolve civil disputes, and to enforce their rights against abuse by powerful state or private interests. First and foremost this requires a sufficient number and geographical spread of courts for the population to reach them, and provisions made for all citizens to understand the proceedings. Improvements in the management and organisation of courts can go a long way toward facilitating the use of the courts, including help desks and information kiosks that enable citizens to access information about their cases and about the court proceedings. The work required to create or improve a nation's court system is difficult and long, and many past projects have not delivered for the poor.

In 2004 the Government of Serbia began introducing an automated case management system in its commercial court system, long a bastion of corruption. The new system selected judges at random, charged litigants standard fees, and allowed citizens to track the progress of their cases online. The resulting increase in transparency, efficiency, and fairness caused a 24 percent reduction in the inventory of pending cases during 2006, and, between 2004 and 2006 a 38 percent reduction in the time needed to enforce a contract.

However, a number of successful projects have been undertaken, especially in middle-income countries, which served to increase the impartiality, speed, and reliability of court systems.

Encourage courts to give due consideration to the interests of the poor

Courts in both common-law and civil-law countries have found new ways to redress injustice. Judges are capable of making all human rights – civil and political, as well as economic, social, and cultural – subject to law. Social action litigation and public interest law in South Asia and South Africa has shown how to empower courts to become an institutional voice for the poor. These innovations should be recognised and incorporated into policies for improving access to justice in all countries.[68] Enabling judiciaries to apply international human-rights norms and standards when adjudicating disputes arising under national or domestic law will go a long way towards making the legal system more capable of empowering the poor.

Improve informal and customary dispute resolution

Although much of the focus of the legal empowerment agenda is on how to achieve empowerment through the formal institutions of the state, the vast majority of the world's poor rely on non-state, informal justice systems. Therefore, it is vitally important to consider non-state justice. Appropriately structuring the relationship between state and non-state systems is crucial. Reforms in pluralistic legal systems might include combining formal or tacit recognition of the non-state justice system with education and awareness campaigns that promote evolution of the informal legal system. Targeted constraints on the non-

state system are also important, in particular in regard to limits on practices that perpetuate the subordination of women. These systems may also be strengthened with the support of civil society and community-based organisations.

In many contexts, *Third Party Arbitration Courts* (TPACs) can be considered a success. These mechanisms offer effective protection of rights and/or effective resolutions of disputes over contested property arrangements, especially for disenfranchised women. In general, the success of alternative dispute resolution depends on certain standards and practices, such as the right of poor people to appoint judges of their choice for the dispute resolution. But it is equally imperative that the alternative dispute resolution mechanisms are recognised as legitimate and linked to formal enforcement, and that they do not operate totally outside the realm of the legal system.[69]

Enable self-help with information and community organising

While there is a certain tendency to equate

access to justice with access to legal services, on the assumption that the only road to justice leads through lawyers and courts, often a poor person's first (and sometimes only) option is to see what she can do for herself. Empowering the poor through improved dissemination of legal information and formation of peer groups (self-help) are first-step strategies towards justice. Poor people may not receive the protection or opportunities to which they are legally entitled because they do not know the law or do not know how to go about securing the assistance of someone who can provide the necessary help. Modern information and communication technologies are particularly well suited to support interventions geared towards strengthening information-sharing groups, teaching the poor about their rights, and encouraging non-formal legal education.

An Agenda for Property Rights
Promote an inclusive property rights system

An inclusive pro-poor property-rights system

requires rules that clearly define the bundle of rights and obligations between people and assets. Property law should offer clear and simple options of legal personality and corporate ownership for small businesses and customary associations of the poor. Legal protection of limited liability has to be extended to poor micro-entrepreneurs, and adverse possession rights formally recognised for their real as well as intangible assets. Legal frameworks enabling housing and land associations should be promoted, allowing individual and common property to be combined by people with limited assets. Officially recognised property documentation should take the form of simple certificates that grant formal recognition to social practices and customary tenure.

The state should enhance the asset base of the poor by enabling community-based ownership. In some legal cultures community-based ownership in natural resources such as grazing lands, forests, water, fisheries, and surface minerals are traditional and effective ways to grant control and proprietary rights to persons who have little or no other property. These systems should be both recognised and fully protected against arbitrary seizure. At the same time communities should be given the option to recognise individual property rights within the community and extend them to outsiders. But, depending on the context, if private operators want to exploit these resources, and/or seek to take them out of communal control, while the affected community depends upon the resources for their lives and destiny, the state may have an interest to intervene, at the request and on behalf of this community. In general, the use of natural resources must be regulated by clear and predictable rules and standards that are applicable, not only to the community but also to private owners.

Efforts should be made to secure the property rights of urban shanty dwellers and rural state land squatters by using a range of measures including financial mechanisms, granting them adequate documentation to their already occupied lands, or by providing them suitable alternatives. Rental markets often provide the first step out of landlessness for the poor. More robust and transparent guarantees should strengthen the position of the rural and urban poor in rental arrangements. By virtue of marriage or free union, real and moveable property held or bought by the male partner should automatically be considered the co-property of the woman. Inheritance rules have to provide for male and female heirs to receive equal consideration in testamentary distributions so as to prevent the disinheritance of women and girls. Divorce laws must also treat men and women equally.

Promoting a truly inclusive property-rights system that incorporates measures to strengthen tenure security requires learning from the mixed experience with past individual titling programmes. To ensure protection and inclusion of the poorest, a broad range of policy measures should be considered. These include formal recognition, adequate representation, and integration of a variety of forms of land tenure such as customary rights, indigenous peoples' rights, group rights, and certificates. Success depends greatly upon comprehensively reforming the governance system surrounding property rights, as explored below. These systems need to be accessible, affordable, transparent, and free from unnecessary complexity. Above all, the poor must be protected from arbitrary eviction by due process and full compensation. Reforms must be accompanied by innovative mechanisms of social policy, including the provision of affordable finance for housing, livelihoods, infrastructure, and basic services. Conducting state land audits and publishing the findings can help reduce the opportunities for the grabbing of public land.

Institutionalise an effective property rights governance system

The functioning of the property administration agency and land administration bodies is critical for the poor. Rules are resources that can easily be subverted to serve the interests of the few, for example through corruption and lack of transparency. Hence, the governance structure and performance of such systems should be reviewed and, as necessary, reformed. The separation of the powers of land registration and public land management is one such reform that will reduce the risk of abusive practices. In addition, property administration agencies should have offices easily accessible to the poor, and, in general, decentralised and accountable land-management and governance systems should be promoted, especially where they can build on traditional mechanisms such as of conflict resolution. The time and cost of formally registering property should be slashed. To ensure that a nation's property is recognised and legally enforceable by law, all owners must have access to the same rights and standards. This would allow bringing the extralegal economy into the formal economy systematically and massively.

The number of steps buyers and sellers must follow to formally transfer property should be kept to a minimum. The responsibilities of various levels of government in managing public land should be clearly defined. Strict

In the lowlands of eastern Bolivia, land rights lie at the heart of a pioneering agreement to preserve both an indigenous peoples' way of life and a unique tract of dry tropical forest. Negotiations between the Government and the Guarani-Izoceno resulted in two landmark decisions. The first preserved 3.4 million hectares of uninhabited Gran Chaco forest as a national park. The second granted the Guarani-Izoceno title to 1.5 million hectares as a communally owned indigenous territory. For the Guarani-Izoceno, the outcome was a pragmatic compromise in which they relinquished any ownership claim to the Gran Chaco forest but gained sole right to exploit the land and forests of their titled territory.

Source: The Wealth of the Poor 2005

limits should be set on the state's ability to expropriate land. The legal framework should be adequately enforced and sufficiently coherent so that it does not conflict with other property-related laws that would disenfranchise vulnerable groups. Among the laws and codes that should be reviewed for consistency are property laws, land laws, collateral laws, civil codes, family laws and codes, inheritance laws and codes, and marital law and codes.

Manual systems of land registration are highly labour intensive and lead to significant error and duplication. The costs of property certification can be considerably reduced and transparency improved by computerisation and GPS systems, especially where comprehensive records do not yet exist. However, there are three caveats. Corruption can easily increase in the early phase of digitisation, though it can be reduced dramatically once the systems are operational. A crucial step is to validate the data collected at the local level with the people concerned. Secondly there is the danger of over-engineering. Technical solutions are only sustainable if they match the locally available infrastructure, resources, and capacities. Land administration institutions will only be independent from the pressure of powerful social actors if they can sustain their recurrent operations financially. Thirdly, computerisation and technical fixes will do little good if the broader system of property governance remains unreformed and inaccessible to the poor. Technical solutions in the absence of pro-poor legal and institutional reform can do more damage than good.

Property certification has to be complemented by zoning and planning. The formation of ghettoes can be avoided by enforcing mixed land use. Where slums have been formed, it is essential to create a protective and empowering environment of residence and business activity for the poor through special social interest zones. Slum upgrading should include property certification for plots, with a minimum of service development and provision for incremental improvement of infrastructure. This helps to grant the poor sustainable ownership and participation in the value increase of property.

Develop property and credit markets accessible to the poor

A comprehensive and functional property and business system allows land, houses, moveable property, equity shares, and ideas to be transformed into assets that can be leveraged and bought and sold, at rates determined by market forces, in a transparent and accountable way. It should permit the development of financial mechanisms – including credit and insurance – to facilitate transactions and improve economic outcomes.

The market should be structured to enable the poor to make the most of their assets. Guidance on making contracts should be provided, conditions for land purchase that exclude the poor – such as a requirement for formal education in agriculture – should be minimised, and standard sales contracts that the poor can rely on produced. Leasing rules should be kept simple and clear, notaries and fees for small transactions avoided, and new and small landowners exempted from registration fees and taxes. Preferential rights to buy granted to co-owners, neighbours, or lessees of land should be considered provided arbitrary seizures do not result. In addition, ceilings on ownership and sales moratoria are considered a reasonably successful protective practice, provided that they are limited in time and that time is used for legal and financial education.

Recognise moveable property as collateral

There is growing evidence that expanding the number of items that can be used legally as collateral reduces the cost of credit. More people can borrow if more types of property can be used as collateral and credit markets become more competitive. More of the poor would be able to create credit histories without risking land and entire homes. The credit system does not evolve automatically from the formalisation of assets. Catalytic and concerted action by the state and private financial institutions is needed in order to foster access to credit for poor families and small urban and rural producers. A complementary means of supporting pro-poor credit markets is through the creation of moveable property registries.

Reinforce property rights through social and other public policies

The state can do a lot to endow its citizens with property assets – for instance, by providing access to housing ownership for the poor, offering low-interest loans, and distributing state land. Redistributive land reform needs to be complemented by access to basic services, managerial ability, technology, credit, and markets for the new owners. As an alternative to authoritative reallocation of land, community-based land reform projects provide funds to groups of beneficiaries to purchase land. The provision of funds is made available under the condition of a productive purpose and when land markets are sufficiently developed. The procedure is legally less complicated and politically less sensitive than in compulsory acquisition programmes. Legal conditionality regarding the beneficiaries allows for the pursuit of other social purposes, such as the distribution of purchased land in the name of women.

The extent of household awareness and information on rights has a significantly positive impact on land-related investments and productivity. Only a minority of poor land users is aware of relevant legal provisions. This implies that the lion's share of the associated productivity gains of property certification remains to be realised through education and information.

Multiple consultations and involvement of social organisations contribute to a shift in the power equation and to increased satisfaction and efficiency of property reform. In particular, active communication with, and participation by, civil society are important to ensure the quality of systemic change in the property-rights regime. On a broader scale, such measures contribute to the fostering of citizenship and social cohesion.

Housing production employs local labour, re-circulates income into the local economy, and contributes to the development of skilled labour. The government can play a catalytic role in housing promotion by providing credit, and by bringing together the private sector and other civil society organisations of the poor to foster conditions that favour the development of pro-poor housing and, ultimately, ownership by the poor.

Lastly, the government can also play the role of intermediary in negotiations between the owner of the land and its low income occupiers in situations where the original land owners have little hope of recovering their occupied property without prolonged litigation, and where getting even a part of the land back has major advantages.

An Agenda for Labour Rights

Ultimately, the aim of labour rights is to ensure freely chosen and productive work, carried out in conditions of freedom, dignity, and equality – what is summed up as the 'decent work agenda.' The specific content of the decent work agenda, which has been accepted as a global goal,[70] is best defined in each country through social dialogue. The aim should be to make employment a central goal of economic policies, and to provide gradual improvements in the quality of work and returns to labour, including through the effective enforcement of labour rights, as a main route out of poverty.

Institutions that help to create jobs, improve labour regulations, and enforce fundamental principles and rights at work, need to be strengthened in order to create synergies between the protection of the working poor, their productivity, and that of their assets. Institutions and regulations should be reviewed to examine their impacts on wealth creation and labour protection.

Many voluntary codes of conduct refer to fundamental principles and rights at work, such as

India © ILO / M. Crozet

the prohibition of forced labour, child labour, and discrimination at work, which are based on ILO core labour standards. They are important tools for motivating multinational corporations to improve their performance, and are already playing an important role in strengthening labour rights, as businesses have become more sensitive to ethical consumer reactions. Efforts to strengthen labour rights should focus on the following:

In Kenya, both cash transfers and job programmes help enhance people's capabilities, particularly children's. Cash transfers that increase the income of poor households may be enough to improve children's education and health if there is an adequate supply of such services. But a job programme is likely to have a stronger multiplier impact than child grants if it helps to develop economic and social infrastructure. If such a programme involves building health clinics and schools, for instance, it can boost the supply of social services.

Source: International Poverty Center 2007

Strengthen identity, voice, representation, and dialogue

The process of legal empowerment starts with identity. Just as property and physical assets of the poor are recognised so too must the greatest asset of the poor, namely their labour and human capital, be effectively recognised. There is a particular need to ensure that workers and entrepreneurs in the informal economy have the right to freedom of association through organisations of their own choosing and to collective bargaining, particularly women and youth who are over-represented in the informal economy. Emphasis should be placed on building up representative organisations of the working poor, particularly of wage and self-employed workers operating in the informal economy, to have voice, representation, and dialogue with formal economy operators and with public authorities in order to defend their rights.

Strengthen the quality of labour regulation and the effective enforcement of fundamental principles and rights at work

The purpose is to create synergy between protection and productivity of the working poor and of their assets. Reviewing the quality of institutions and regulation should involve a critical and self-critical review of legal instruments from the point of view of their impacts on productivity and on the protection of labour.

Support minimum package of labour rights for workers in the informal economy

A minimum package of labour rights should be established and enforced for the working poor in the informal economy with gradual and progressive convergence of labour rights applying to all workers. This should uphold and go beyond the Declaration on Fundamental Principles and Rights at Work with three crucial additional aspects relating to working conditions: health and safety at work, hours of work, and minimum income. Such a minimum floor for empowerment must be realistic and enforceable. Progress towards a fuller set of labour rights should be expected.

Strengthen access to opportunities

Policies to create and provide improved access of the poor to new opportunities for full, productive and freely chosen employment, as promoted in ILO Convention 122, can provide a key mechanism for empowering the poor in the informal economy, and facilitating their transition to formality. Opportunities for education and capacity building, as well as measures for combating discrimination, help increase legal recognition of the poor and also bring them closer to new economic opportunities.

Support inclusive social protection

The recognition of the right to social security has been developed through universally accepted instruments, such as the Universal Declaration of Human Rights and the International Covenant on Economic Social and Cultural Rights, which proclaim that social security is a fundamental societal right to which every human is entitled. This must be upheld by all countries through laws, institutions, and responsive mechanisms that can protect the poor from shocks and contingencies that can impoverish, and measures that guarantee access to medical care, health insurance, old age pensions, and social services. These mechanisms must not be solely dependent on the evidence of employment status but must be open to all types of workers. From a systemic perspective rights to pensions and health protection should be granted to the people as citizens rather than as workers and awarded on universal principles.

Promote gender equality

Poverty has a gender dimension, and legal empowerment can help drive gender equality. A key challenge is to ensure that ILO labour standards, which promote equality of opportunity and treatment, are effectively extended to informal sector workers.[71] The starting point for this process lies in the core labour standards on gender equality. Useful guidance can be found in the 1996 ILO Home Work Convention,[72] which mandates the extension of legal protection and legal empowerment to home workers (industrial outworkers who work from their homes), who are predominantly women.

An Agenda for Business Rights

Many developing countries are emerging from a history of heavy-handed regulation, with approvals required for even the smallest

Over 90 percent of India's workers are in the informal economy (including agricultural workers), with little – if any – statutory social security. Most are casual labourers, contract and piece-rate workers and self-employed own-account workers. The Government of India recently launched the Unorganised Sector Workers' Social Security Scheme in 50 districts on a pilot basis. The scheme provides for three basic protections: old age pension, personal accident insurance, and medical insurance. It is compulsory for registered employees and voluntary for self-employed workers. Workers contribute to the scheme, as do employers. Where self-employed workers join the scheme they pay worker and employer contributions. Government also contributes. Workers Facilitation Centres are being set up to assist workers (see above under Securing Rights of Informal Workers). The scheme will be administered through the already existing Employee Provident Fund Organisation offices around the country. Source: Government of India, 2004

choose low-risk businesses that often yield low returns. They operate with a limited amount of capital and, as a result, are forced to do business on a very small scale. Since they hardly ever accumulate capital, it is often very difficult for these entrepreneurs to sell the business and profit from both the tangible and intangible assets they have accumulated.[73]

Economic policies and commercial law, which in the great majority of poor countries are most often geared to large enterprises, have to change to become inclusive of the vast numbers of business owners at the base of the economic pyramid. Reform of these policies and legal frameworks should focus on helping informal businesses use all of their assets to operate productive and profitable enterprises. Key elements in efforts to achieve these aims include:

activity, and an overly centralised and inflexible authority. Poor quality law making over the years has created a tangle of complex and inconsistent laws that present a daunting regulatory hurdle to the would-be formal enterprise. As such, the regulatory systems of these countries are not developed to support a flourishing market economy that will create growth and formal jobs.

Under these circumstances, small informal businesses must often assume bigger risks than the larger and usually formal firms, and spend more time and resources to monitor their agents and partners, which explains why they usually hire relatives and close friends. They frequently

A package of business rights underlined in policies, and instituted and enforced through regulatory bodies.

Irrespective of their size or growth potential, the rights of all those operating informal businesses must be recognised. These include the right to work and to incorporate a business, which necessitates the ability to vend, occupy a workplace, and access basic infrastructure such as shelter, electricity, water, and sanitation. As informal businesses grow they will need additional legal rights and protections, such as the ability to obtain tax breaks, export licenses, and access to services like transport and communications. Efforts to strengthen basic business rights must

be based on an in-depth knowledge of local practices, and, where possible, incorporating them into the legal framework. Creating mechanisms and financing to provide social protection to informal entrepreneurs is also important, as are legal mechanisms that help people operate and expand their businesses once they have entered the market. Absence of commercial rights, including rules relating to entity shielding, limited liability and capital lock-in, and perpetual succession of the firm as well as manager and employee liability rights and protection of minority shareholders, increases the likelihood of businesses returning to informality.

Streamlined administrative procedures

Administrative barriers are the bureaucratic requirements that flow from regulations, their implementation, and enforcement. A regulation may be well designed, proportionate, and efficient, but its true effect on enterprises comes from the way in which it is administered. Administrative barriers are the hassle that dis-

suades informal enterprises from wanting to interact with government officials[74]. The regulations imposed on business fall into several categories. Some regulations governing business start-ups raise the costs of entering the formal sector. Other regulations govern ongoing business activity, and still others affect closing a business. The central authority dictates some of these regulations while regional or municipal governments determine others. Furthermore, small businesses face government-imposed costs in the areas of labour practices, payroll charges, health and safety standards, taxation, and foreign trade.

The time and money spent complying with government regulations imposes burdensome transaction costs on businesses. In addition, the direct cost of payments, such as licensing fees, also represents a significant cost of doing business. Conversely, payments made to avoid detection of non-compliance, or payoffs to government officials, are the costs of operating in the informal sector.

The red tape and costs involved in registering or obtaining licenses for a business need to be slashed and all business owners need to be given easy access.

Broadened access to financial services and support innovation in financial products

Access to finance is essential for businesses. However, businesses in the informal economy lack access to financial markets and the capacity to compete in product markets. Improved access to basic financial services consisting of savings, credit, insurance, pensions, and tools for risk management, is a critical input for emerging and potential entrepreneurs to leverage economic opportunities and improve their quality of life.

More inclusive financial markets require that there be awareness in both formal and informal credit systems of the way the working poor use credit, and the barriers and inappropriate rules in formal lending procedures. They also require having in place legal and administrative processes that make the processing of collateral –including moveable property as well as social collateral – cheaper, transparent, and faster. It is also necessary to give support to innovation in financial products and services, with a view to deepening their outreach.

Consultation, participation, and inclusive rule-setting

Informal businesses and their representatives need to be consulted and to participate in relevant policymaking and rule-setting bodies. They need to be kept informed of their legal rights so that they can bargain effectively, enforce contracts, and seek redress. The legal empowerment agenda for business rights emphasises reforms to provide a legal and institutional environment, and the rule of law, which

will enable poor business owners to develop their capacity and to use their talent, energy, and initiative to build up their assets and to generate efficient and productive enterprises.

Business reforms combined with property reforms can bring security, resources, and increase competitiveness of all firms but particularly micro-, small-, and medium-sized enterprises. Growth of these enterprises greatly enhances the possibilities of strengthening labour rights. The more inclusive and attractive the formal market becomes, the better the chances for regulating labour rights, which in turn helps build the human capital for the next generation. As Ireland and Spain have shown in recent history, there is tremendous potential in bringing policymakers and SME entrepreneurs together to develop strategies along these lines.

Making legal empowerment relevant and astute strategy. It is time for a new approach of laws and human rights in the lives of the poor.

5
Implementation
Strategies

a reality requires a politically
based on knowledge…
that builds on the bedrock
to give them real meaning

L egal Empowerment of the Poor is a bold vision and its implementation is challenging. This chapter sets out how it can be done. Guidelines for implementation, phases, policies, and tactics for national action are outlined. This is followed by an agenda for the international community.

Four billion people live outside the rule of law. Existing political, administrative, and judicial institutions are not geared to protect the rights of the poor. Much of the aid community is in crisis as it comes to acknowledge that old approaches are not good enough. Now is the time to reckon with reality, and strive for new solutions. As Albert Einstein observed, 'We can't solve problems by using the same kind of thinking we used when we created them.' 21st-century solutions are indeed called for to complement or even replace strategies for

poverty reduction and wealth creation that were developed in the last century.

The Commission believes that significant changes in the relations between the state and the poor, and in public – and private – power, are needed. Realising the full potential of legal empowerment ultimately requires establishing more open, inclusive, and accountable institutions across the political and economic system. But everything does not need to happen at once. Legal empowerment can start with a change in some policy areas. As the poor gain income, assets, and power, they will be in a stronger position to call for additional institutional reform.

The overarching frameworks for Legal Empowerment of the Poor, such as the Universal Declaration of Human Rights and other international legal covenants, already exist.[75] The world's governments are committed to them. What are lacking are the myriad national and local rules of the game and policies that give substance to those grand declarations in the everyday lives of the poor. Putting the necessary reforms into practical effect requires sober analysis of what is feasible, but it also needs a readiness to take chances when the timing looks right. Pragmatic policymakers look for policy windows that open and use them to create a space for moving forward to solve the particular problems facing the poor. It is important to recognise that while it will often make sense to anchor the legal empowerment agenda in existing development processes, such as Poverty Reduction Strategies, legal empowerment should not be hidebound by any processes that are stalled or dysfunctional.

Broad political coalitions for pro-poor change that involve leaders from across society are needed to galvanise and sustain reforms and to prevent reforms from being diverted, diluted, or delayed. National contexts differ so a single blueprint for accomplishing this objective does not exist. But certain key conditions and rules should guide implementation of legal empowerment. As Chapter 2 sets out, the four key conditions for legal empowerment are identity, information, voice, and organisation. The five guiding rules are that the process should be bottom-up, affordable, realistic, liberating, and risk aware.

There is revealing comparative experience from countries that have carried out pro-poor legal and regulatory reforms. The Commission's working groups have painstakingly collected evidence from around the world about what works and what does not. Their reports analyse why and how, and set out promising approaches involving governments, public-private partner-

ships, civil-society organisations, and innovative social movements, which can be modified and applied to a wide variety of settings.[76] The most common mistakes are to underestimate the impediments to implementation and to not foresee unintended negative consequences for the poor. Success, on the other hand, invariably involves understanding the impediments and addressing them, listening to the poor, and learning by doing. Because these processes do not work across societies in exactly the same ways, policymakers must be watchful and experimental. Whatever type of reform is chosen should be phased to mesh with society's unique past and its readiness to accept change.

To kick-start as controversial and deep-seated a change as legal empowerment – an approach that threatens many vested interests – the positive role of national political leadership cannot be overstated. Pursuing a particular policy, such as expanding access to justice, requires a handful of leaders who agree on what the problem is and how to solve it. Some of these individuals may emerge as 'policy champions' who drive reform forward by marshalling a broader coalition for change within government, and by overcoming objections and obstacles.

Getting it Right From the Start

Before proceeding very far with legal empowerment activities, a contextual analysis must be done to establish what reforms are most in demand and which have the greatest likelihood of success. Such an analysis would also give guidance to the implementation process, and tell reformers which risks need to be mitigated, and which challenges must be addressed. This improves the likelihood of success. The focus should be on social and cultural factors potentially affecting implementation, on the

Implementation of Legal Empowerment

The way in which legal empowerment is designed, implemented, and monitored, is distinctive. It is a bottom-up approach in the sense that it is based in the realities of poverty and exclusion as experienced by the poor, and requires their active participation and buy-in. At the same time, legal empowerment requires political leadership and commitment from the top and alliances with key stakeholders. It is a political approach based on broad coalitions for change, rather than a technical or bureaucratic approach that engages only with international civil servants, government leaders, and elites. Above all, while legal empowerment is buttressed by international human-rights principles, its priorities are set by the poor and grounded in local needs and conditions. New indicators, indices, and monitoring and evaluation protocols will be necessary to match the distinctive nature of Legal Empowerment of the Poor.

The Commission has identified five characteristics that together distinguish legal empowerment from traditional approaches to legal and institutional reform:

Bottom-up and pro-poor

The legal empowerment process should be based on the needs of the poor as they themselves experience and express them. Reforms must be designed and implemented in an inclusive and participatory way, and geared towards helping the poor organise themselves to get out of poverty.

Affordable

Measures proposed, procedures agreed, and requirements imposed, must all be within the means of the poor that they seek to benefit.

Realistic

Reforms should be based on a realistic understanding of formal and informal mechanisms, norms, and institutions, and how they interrelate and interact. Governments need to engage with poor people to find out how and why grass-roots institutions work, as well as their strengths and weaknesses. Unconventional mechanisms for gathering information may be needed.

Liberating

Legal empowerment should focus on removing legal barriers that hinder the economic activities of the poor. Since this is inextricably linked to a functioning regulatory and institutional framework, the burden of proof for such requirements lies with the state.

Risk aware

Care must be taken in designing, implementing, and monitoring local reforms. Inevitably, though, ambitious reforms may unintentionally harm some poor and vulnerable people. These risks should be scrupulously monitored throughout the process.

---

economic context – which can also both help and hinder – and on the openness and capacity of the state. Supplementing the inventory of these concerns should be a careful analysis of the reach and hold that informal institutions have on the poor. The full contextual analysis is the basis for a feasibility review of various empowerment scenarios. The most important elements of such an analysis are:

- The domestic social structure, especially its gender, class, and ethnic makeup, plus cultural attitudes toward participation and equality;
- The economic context – including the distribution of wealth and income, and the level and rate of economic growth;
- The characteristics of the state – both the political and the administrative system;
- The extent of economic and political informality and tensions with the formal and officially recognised systems.

Contextual analysis and knowledge of the policy environment are essential to estimate whether conditions appear ripe for extensive or modest legal empowerment reforms, which implementation options seem most probable, what sequencing and timelines for reform are best, how the reforms should be designed, what tradeoffs need to be considered, which risk-mitigating mechanisms are worth trying, and what variables need special monitoring during implementation.

Many societies and cultures have hierarchical and patriarchal power structures that make carrying out legal empowerment difficult. Involving the poor in decision-making and giving women equal rights may be particularly challenging. In some contexts, custom may run contrary to a vision of human rights enshrined in a national constitution, particularly where it comes to the treatment of women and minorities. A similar dilemma arises when attempting to ensure minimum levels of accountability and transparency within customary structures. Fortunately, customs are not rigid and unchanging. It is thus possible to aim at a process in which customary practices evolve in response to social development and human rights principles. [77]

These shifting informal mechanisms exist partly because they are often more accessible and helpful to poor people than the official institutions in many instances. They encourage flexibility and compromise within community norms. In other cases, the informal system is neither efficient nor fair. Context is critical.

The distribution of power and wealth also matters for legal empowerment. If ownership of land, capital, and other productive assets

South Africa's minibus and taxi industry shows how informal institutions that spring up in the absence of effective government regulation can end up being harmful. Minibuses and taxis are the main means of transport for South Africa's poor. A loophole in the transit law allowed this largely unregulated sector to emerge toward the end of the apartheid era. Independent micro-business operators came to dominate the sector over time. In the absence of government regulation, individual taxi owner-drivers turned to fledgling private industry associations to allocate taxi routes and cab stands, and settle disputes among competitors. These associations soon grew very powerful in their own right and began to fight turf wars. By the mid-1990s a virtual taxi war was costing hundreds of drivers and passengers their lives each year.

Source: Barrett 2003

are highly concentrated, reformers have to be cautious about regularising the system of economic rights. Entrenching existing inequalities in ownership will negate the value of reform for the poor and can even lead to further marginalisation. On the other hand, perpetuating exclusion from formal ownership due to unequal distribution of land and other assets may be an even worse option. Judgement must be married to context.

The effectiveness of state institutions is another contextual factor. How capable is public administration? This is related to corruption, capacity to deliver, and ability to protect citizens and their assets. In many countries laws favourable to the poor exist, but are not implemented. Where the state is not effective its residents must protect assets and resolve disputes pragmatically, by aligning with a political patron,

Cambodia © Jean-Luc Fievet 2007

for instance. This will often hamper legal empowerment. In fragile states the capacity is even weaker. The legal system is particularly ineffective in such societies. The good news is that once the importance of legal reforms and governance functions for legal empowerment is understood, the investment required to strengthen these functions can often be mobilised. The intensity required may be one of effort rather than money.

Managing Stakeholders and Mobilising Allies

Along with knowledge of context, a second important early task in implementation is stakeholder analysis. Stakeholders are interested parties with the capacity to advance or hinder a policy change. Their position is determined by their perceived interests and they may or may not be formally or self-consciously organised.[78] It is crucial to differentiate among constituencies, to better understand the divisions, alliances and particular needs. Stakeholders who might oppose or assist with legal empowerment need to be scrutinised to establish how they can become supporters of the process. The purpose is to get a firmer grasp of the probability of succeeding with legal empowerment reforms, managing the stakeholders, and establishing what it takes to build a minimum winning coalition for legal empowerment in the country.

In Beijing, law enforcement officers and local authorities look the other way when rural-urban migrant entrepreneurs who do not comply fully with licensing requirements lease licenses illegally from local residents. This illicit trade survives because bureaucrats profit from it. Streamlining business registration in line with legal empowerment goals would threaten illegal but routine bureaucratic income in the Chinese capital.

Source: He 2005

The poor are the intended beneficiaries of legal-empowerment policies. A legal or organisational change that looks self-evidently beneficial to experts from the outside may be seen as too risky or not worth doing from the perspective of someone inside the poor community. That is why the poor must have a hand in implementation. Empowerment strategies depend on the beneficiary stakeholders choosing to go along. If the poor resist a change, the best-intended policy will do little good. The principal allies of the poor are pro-poor community associations and civil-society activists. They can be mobilised for reform and become strong allies. Some may be local social action or advocacy groups, such as the Indonesian Legal Aid Foundation, whose mission is to defend poor people in court and expand their rights. Others include professional associations sympathetic to the plight of the excluded. Ecuador's Association of Law School Deans, for example, supports legal assistance for the indigent in that country.

Legal empowerment will in some cases also create policy 'losers.' One example is redistribution of a right or benefit from one group of stakeholders to another when there are mutually exclusive claims to a fixed resource such as fertile land or minerals. Landlords, shopkeepers, moneylenders, and other local elites may see a threat from disenfranchised people exercising new rights or reviving latent ones. Professionals may also have a stake in maintaining the disempowering status quo, such as lawyers who would lose out if laws were translated into everyday language or if inexpensive means of conflict resolution spread. Policymakers may endeavour to minimise redistributive conflicts by expanding economic opportunities so that different interests can be negotiated to meet the needs of every side, but plenty of potential for confrontation remains as long as important stakeholders believe others'

gains come at their expense. This may be linked to the fact that the mutual payoff to legal empowerment is in the future, and not now.

Resistance may also come from government officials, court officers, and others who interpret and administer laws, statutes, and regulations. Permits, business licenses, tax assessments, and the like are sources of power and potential illegal income through bribes, kickbacks, and other 'rent-seeking' behaviour. Government officials who gain from these policies and legal instruments may sabotage reform. Where possible, they should be given positive incentives to support legal empowerment policies instead of resisting them – for example by offering civil servants promotions, interesting new responsibilities, training opportunities, or other perquisites if they help with implementation.

Instead of trying to block reforms outright, powerful economic actors may subtly manipulate them to their advantage – a phenomenon known as 'elite capture.'[79] In many countries, for example, speculators pre-empt prospective titling programmes by buying up land from squatters at prices slightly higher than prevailing informal ones. Squatters benefit in the short term, but miss out on the main benefits of the titling programme, which accrue to the people with deeper pockets.[80] The sequential and conditional release of funds is one strategy for countering the persistent problem of elite capture.

Collective counteraction by the poor, to secure their rights in the face of resistance, is difficult. Even if potential policy losers are a minority, such as a handful of large landholders or government bureaucrats, they will tend to organise effectively to defend their vested interests. Prospective winners may not be aware of what they might gain and may rightly fear that they will lose out if change does not happen quickly. Hence, mobilisation of allies and supportive stakeholders, and finding ways to manage the critical ones, is fundamental. Success is most reliably won when one delivers measurable and meaningful benefits to the beneficiaries.

Action at the International Level

Most current and past poverty reduction strategies were designed on the basis of economic growth and trickle down, or on redistribution. Governments were supported to enhance their capacities to provide public goods and services, including health and education, security and

The UN Global Compact

Some larger businesses and multinational corporations are less adversarial about legal empowerment and might sometimes be policy allies. Over 3,000 companies in more than 100 countries have joined the UN's Global Compact, which commits them to support high standards in areas such as human rights and labour. These firms often say that they would like to forge partnerships with poor communities in the developing world to create business models that are sustainable, equitable, and embedded in the local culture.

Sources: UN 2007 and Hart 2005

stability, and a macroeconomic environment to stimulate growth and investment. This continues to be necessary, but it is not sufficient. More equitable distribution of opportunities for participation of the poor in growth has been aspired to, but remains largely unrealised. This is because of structural and institutional

arrangements that have not been working for the large majority of people, most of whom have had to seek refuge in the informal sector to eke out a living.

While commendable efforts to improve the coherence and effectiveness of development aid, such as the Paris Declaration, are underway, these are slow to materialise on the ground. Stronger action to meet harmonisation and alignment goals is needed. Aid Effectiveness and Legal Empowerment of the Poor must complement each other. Therefore the agenda for Legal Empowerment of the Poor should be pursued in key development corporation fora such as the OECD-DAC, the UN Development Cooperation Forum, and the annual meetings of the Bretton Woods institutions. The rapid growth in South-South cooperation presents promising opportunities and new arenas for legal empowerment.

The expanding reach of transnational non-state actors, such as large corporations and civil society and community-based organisations, is now undeniable. For too long, the international community has failed to recognise the true extent of its influence, particularly on norms and standards. Engaging private sector players is crucial as they have the capacity to act at a pace and scale that neither governments nor international agencies can equal.[81] But such advantages do not come without risks; for example, respect for human, economic, and social rights must not fall prey to short-term profit considerations.

Likewise, the spheres of influence of civil

Phases in the Legal Empowerment Process

The policy environment in a country should inform the strategy and design of reform implementation. To be able to make legal empowerment a reality for the poor, comprehensive reforms are necessary. Such reforms can start with change in some policy areas, and be sequenced and implemented in phases. Lessons learnt from the implementation of other complex reforms show that the generic phases listed in the text box below are particularly useful tools.

Legal empowerment involves a complex combination of technical, institutional, and political changes. The following sets of tasks are important – the specific sequencing will vary by country and context, but the design of each component should be based on the principles of adaptation to user needs and availability of resources, user participation, parsimony (the least amount of information and cost required to accomplish the task), and simplicity.

Agenda setting: Advocate for change, develop policy issues, and make decisions that launch policy reforms. Politicians and interest groups tend to take the lead in these activities, but they will seldom succeed without mobilisation of the poor. A detailed assessment of the issues to be addressed should be included. The analysis will identify policy, legal, and institutional concerns, as well as gaps in resources, capacity, and tools.

Policy formulation and legitimisation: Address the technical content of reform measures. However, besides technical content, reform measures need to be accepted and seen as necessary and important. The poor should, through their representatives, be part of the reform design process. Critical issues include sequencing and timing, resource constraints, establishing a monitoring and evaluation framework, and ensuring a balance between process and products to maintain momentum.

Constituency building: Convince beneficiaries of the advantages of reforms, and demonstrate that long-term benefits are worth short-term costs. Key issues include coordination mechanisms, adoption of a protocol or agreement, clarification of roles and responsibilities, and agreement on a broad process for reform.

Resource mobilisation: Ensure the flow of adequate resources by addressing incentives, and exercising leadership in galvanizing constituencies. Financial, technical, and human resource commitments are needed.

Implementation design and development of organisational capacity: Reformers need to create and nurture networks and partnerships for cooperation and coordination, and provide for the development of new organisational skills and capacities in the public, private, and non-governmental sectors. Old procedures, operating routines, and communication patterns die hard; change is likely to be resisted within some quarters.

Planning action and monitoring progress: Set up systems and procedures for obtaining feedback so that implementation is related to learning and adaptation, in order to produce results and make an impact. Engage implementing parties and beneficiaries in the drawing up of monitoring systems and methodologies, and obtain feedback. This will simplify the process of tracking previously identified indicators. Focus group discussions, workshops, and similar methods can be used to ensure participation.

---

society and community-based organisations are widening. An approach worthy of the 21st century must recognise the immense contributions to change such organisations can bring. To think that the necessary change can be achieved without these players would be misguided.

This year marks the 60th anniversary of the Universal Declaration of Human Rights. It is a momentous occasion, and an exceptional opportunity to harness the political power of the moment to make a lasting difference.

The Declaration has been remarkably successful. Few ideas are now as powerful as human rights. Crowds rally to demand them, millions pen letters in support of them, some are willing to risk their lives for them, and even despots pay lip service to them. Virtually all states subscribe to the Declaration, the two Covenants and the Geneva Conventions, and most make a serious attempt to abide by them.

Yet, in many respects, the promise of human rights remains unfulfilled. The fine words of Article 1 of the Universal Declaration, 'All human beings are born free and equal in

While not advocating a 'Machiavellian approach' to legal empowerment, the old master may still give us relevant insights into the challenge: 'It must be considered that there is nothing more difficult to carry out, nor more doubtful of success, nor more dangerous to handle, than to initiate a new order of things. For the reformer has enemies in all those who profit by the old order, and only lukewarm defenders in all those who would profit by the new order, this lukewarmness arising partly from fear of their adversaries, who have the laws in their favour; and partly from the incredulity of mankind, who do not truly believe in anything new until they have had actual experience of it. Thus it arises that on every opportunity for attacking the reformer, his opponents do so with the zeal of partisans, the others only defend him half-heartedly, so that between them he runs great danger.'

Niccolo Machiavelli

dignity and rights,' ring hollow for someone like Margaret in the Kibera slum. Legal empowerment could make them resonate loud and clear. It is time for a new approach that builds on the bedrock of existing laws and the broad-based support for human rights to give real meaning to them in the everyday lives of the poor. With its focus on working from the bottom up and building a broad coalition for political change tailored to local needs and conditions, legal empowerment offers an essential complement to the traditional top-down approach to human rights.

The Commission calls on the United Nations and the broader multilateral system at the global, regional, and country level, to make Legal Empowerment of the Poor a core mission for the coming decade. Far from replacing the human-rights agenda, it can energise it and drive advances that would otherwise be out of reach. Nor is it a substitute for the MDGs agenda and the quest to eradicate poverty; rather, it enriches these efforts with tools and approaches that attack deep and structural causes of poverty and exclusion. An internationally scaled-up effort to meet the MDGs, coupled with real commitment to legal empowerment, can constitute a powerful and dynamic agenda for an accelerated assault on global poverty, between now and 2015, as well as beyond.

The Commission has achieved consensus on a set of recommendations and principles that it believes should guide and inform global, regional, and national efforts to advance the Legal Empowerment of the Poor, with a strong focus on action where it counts, namely locally and nationally. We seek to raise awareness of its importance and to mobilise governments, intergovernmental institutions, the private sector, and civil society to act, but we cannot – and do not wish to – dictate what should be done. Success in public policy requires full ownership by its principal custodians, namely governments and political leaders. Legal empowerment inherently requires a broad-based, bottom-up approach.

The global agenda that the Commission proposes focuses on building political ownership and supporting local and national reform processes, based on solid empirical and analytical knowledge. Making legal empowerment a political priority requires a politically relevant and astute strategy. A coalition of countries from North and South should volunteer to champion the legal empowerment agenda in the UN leading to UN General Assembly debate and resolution in the 63rd session starting in September 2008.

Establish a global legal empowerment 'open access' arena

The Commission calls on multilateral agencies, foundations, grassroots movements and other civil-society organisations, information and communications firms, and other private-sector entities, to jointly establish a global forum and virtual arena for Legal Empowerment of the Poor. Such a forum, modelled on web-based social and professional networks and communities, would seek to be truly accessible and inclusive, allowing interested people all over the world to interact. A global meeting, at set intervals and combining a major gathering in a physical location with virtual participation around the world, should be established to raise awareness and take stock of progress worldwide.

Develop political consensus regionally – A Regional Compact on Legal Empowerment of the Poor

The Commission believes that regional and

sub-regional political bodies (such as the African Union, ECOWAS, ASEAN, SAFTA, OAS, and Mercosur) should be central to the legal empowerment process. We call on these various bodies to start a dialogue on legal empowerment among their members, using the principles and recommendations of the Commission as a frame of reference. Support can be provided by relevant UN agencies and regionally based Commission members as needed and requested. The European Union's Neighbourhood Policy, which offers EU neighbours a privileged relationship, building upon a mutual commitment to common values, could serve as an inspiration for such a regional compact.

Regional bodies should be encouraged to develop their own outputs such as:
- Guidance and best-practice documents for their members;
- Binding policy documents with standards and criteria for national implementation;
- Regional cooperation programmes;
- Common statistical standards, indicator sets, and targets.

These are likely to differ from region to region, but would be based on broad consensus within each region, and build on universal economic and social rights. Regions could seek to formulate a Regional Legal Empowerment Compact involving key stakeholders within the region, and comprising some or all of the above four elements.

Provide coherent support to legal empowerment efforts at the country level

Some countries are already trying to build a more inclusive legal order that provides better opportunities for the poor and the excluded. The Commission urges relevant multilateral agencies and other actors to provide more and faster policy and technical support to such initiatives when requested. As a first step, multilateral agencies should table the principles and recommendations of this report for discussion with the aim of generating a shared global policy agenda (while allowing for different views and approaches within such a framework). A coherent global policy agenda could lead to the establishment of aligned programmes of investment and technical assistance, based on clear allocation of functions and responsibilities. A similar process can be envisaged among interested donor countries and international non-governmental organisations. The process should draw from the complementarities of the Aid Effectiveness, Financing for Development and Legal Empowerment of the Poor agendas. Policies should evolve over time, based on emerging experiences and lessons learned.

The Commission recommends that dedicated funding mechanisms be established to support regional and country-specific policy and capacity development work. In addition, clear legal empowerment criteria should be introduced into appropriate existing mechanisms. Given their broad development-policy mandates, the Commission calls on UNDP and the World Bank to develop a concrete proposal in this regard, in consultation with other relevant UN departments – such as UN-HABITAT, FAO, and ILO – civil society-organisations, and bilateral donors. UNDP and the World Bank will also develop proposals in which they will encourage a series of country pilots through a process of self-selection. The Commission calls on UNDP to establish and lead a global steering committee or 'friends group' to ensure broad ownership and follow-up

Legal Empowerment Activities

Implementing legal empowerment reforms using such a phased approach calls for a number of different actions and policy measures. The following concrete activities are among them:

Mobilising stakeholders: Once the principle stakeholders have been identified, the relevant ones need to be brought together to agree on a process and a set of principles to guide the legal empowerment agenda. Key requirements include establishment of coordination mechanisms, adoption of a protocol or agreement, clarification of roles and responsibilities, and agreement on a broad process for reform.

Legal empowerment diagnostic: Building on the initial scan of the environment and contextual analysis, a detailed assessment should be made. This diagnostic should focus on both formal and informal institutions, the way they work and their interactions. The analysis will identify policy, legal, and institutional issues, as well as assets and gaps in resources, capacity, and tools.

Action planning: This requires development of the goal, objectives, strategies, and specific interventions that will contribute to the aims of legal empowerment. Critical issues include sequencing and timing, resource constraints, establishing a monitoring and evaluation framework, and ensuring a balance between process and products to maintain momentum.

Pilot activities: These should be built around the idea of 'quick wins' in areas where these are feasible. In this way one can demonstrate some initial success and build the credibility of the legal empowerment agenda.

Scaling-up: Expanding the range of activities and taking on more complicated challenges, will be supported by raising awareness of past successes, additional sensitisation, and strengthening the consultation process.

Institutionalising change and the change process: Advance some of the fundamental reforms by building on the experiences in the pilot phase and scaling-up phase to reform the organisations and rules that shape the institutional context.

of the legal empowerment agenda.

International actors also need to support knowledge accumulation and learning globally, based on emerging experience and evaluations of results and impacts. An important component would be peer-to-peer exchange programmes among and across countries pursuing legal empowerment. In order to build a portfolio with shared characteristics and opportunities for comparison and exchange, such initiatives will have to meet certain eligibility criteria.

The Commission encourages the creation of a small secretariat for coordination and knowledge management, to be housed in UNDP. The inclusion of a wide range of actors will be facilitated through the creation of a knowledge network or community of practice. The global policy and programme agenda for legal empowerment should be increasingly informed and guided by the regional political processes described above, as well as by initiatives and progress at the country level.

Provide for sustained reflection on legal empowerment

Central to human progress, and grounded in many of humanity's most enduring preoccupations, legal empowerment needs not only reflective practitioners, but also the benefit of institutionalised learning. At the junior and local level, school syllabi that introduce children to civic life and human rights, will nurture the child's sense of self and future citizenship. At the international, university level, development curricula and networks of research and teaching need to sustain the intellectual life of legal empowerment, and open the minds of future policymakers. But this is not a straightforward call for yet another specialisation. Professionalised academia is prone to fragmentation, and a hybrid concern such as legal empowerment

should be a small part of drawing the strands together, and for universities recapturing their voice in the public realm. For this, money as well as minds will be needed.

Create innovative mechanisms for legal empowerment support

A series of global instruments could be created, ranging from normative initiatives to operational collaboration and knowledge sharing. Such initiatives need to reflect the political nature of legal empowerment and foster genuine ownership. Rather than creating new institutions or structures, these instruments should be hosted by existing organisations. Global normative initiatives should be sequenced in relation to regional political processes and country-led operational reform efforts, and be directly informed by their outcomes in order to ensure that any global normative framework be securely anchored in actual experience and regional policy processes.

a) Norm setting through a Global Legal Empowerment Compact

While labour rights have been relatively clearly enshrined in international agreements and conventions through the ILO, property and business rights and principles of access to justice, have never been elaborated beyond general references or principles. The Commission recommends that a dialogue on a more comprehensive human rights framework on legal empowerment be initiated. An end result might be a Global Legal Empowerment Compact, ideally based on regionally agreed compacts as described above. Such a compact should be widely understandable, making it evident to the average reader that the core rights of legal empowerment are human rights as important as freedom of speech, the right to vote, and other basic rights. Such a compact would define central principles to which states should subscribe, and give guidelines on how they could be put into practice. In addition to a Compact, or as an alternative, a Declaration on Legal Empowerment could be prepared for consideration by the UN General Assembly. However, the Commission recommends that such a declaration be proposed based on emerging experiences from national, regional, and global initiatives as outlined in this chapter in order to ensure political support and buy-in.

b) Defenders of the Poor

The appointment of 'Defenders of the Poor' could send a powerful signal to poor people around the world that their concerns around legal empowerment can be heard. It could help link the global and local levels in an action-oriented way. At the local or national level, Defenders of the Poor could play an important role in giving poor people a voice and supporting their legal empowerment. The international community could take a decision that such Defenders of the Poor would fall under the concept of human-rights defenders as elaborated in the Declaration on the Rights and Responsibility of Individuals, Groups and Organs of Society to Promote and Protect Universally Recognised Human Rights and Fundamental Freedoms.[82] This would show a very strong commitment by the international community in support of the Defenders of the Poor and protect them in turn from human-rights violations. But also at the Global level there could be Defenders of the Poor. This would be an honorary function with no formal authority and no other task than to continually draw attention to the plight of the poor and the perspective that legal empowerment offers to better their lives. The Global Defenders of the Poor could work at the request of poor peoples' organisations to get issues on the national or international agenda, and to support and publicise solutions to problems and barriers

that poor people face in the areas of property, labour, and business rights. The process would aim to identify and build on local initiatives and find innovative solutions. Initially, some members of the Commission could be asked to serve as global defenders of the poor.

c) Knowledge clearinghouse on legal empowerment

An institution could be given the mandate to provide a clearinghouse for knowledge and experience, openly available to all interested parties. This clearinghouse would draw on policy research, evaluations, project reports, and other relevant materials. Links with existing or newly created academic networks on legal empowerment should serve to promote academic research and agree on a research agenda.

d) Public-private partnerships for legal empowerment

Recognising the complexities of reform and the wide array of functions and services that would be involved, the Commission recommends that imaginative public-private partnerships be established at a global or regional level. These would bring together entities with relevant resources and expertise to support governments and other actors in their efforts to promote legal empowerment. Such partnerships could encompass multilateral agencies, financial institutions, entities involved in mapping and geographic information systems, providers of legal services, community-based and civil-society organisations, foundations, and others.

e) Businesses promoting a legal empowerment agenda

Businesses increasingly influence norms and standards and therefore have an important role to play in promoting the legal empowerment agenda. The UN Global Compact, as the world's

Tactics for Champions and Change Agents

To succeed in implementing legal empowerment reforms, change agents must be mobilised and able to think creatively about how to make policies available, affordable, and acceptable in the specific context in which they work. The following strategic options and tactical considerations may help achieve that goal:

Find your own way: There is a rich base of comparative international experience, but no ready-made formulas, for achieving legal empowerment. Solutions that suit one context may be completely wrong in another.

Think systemically, act incrementally: Empowerment requires systemic changes – big bang approaches are rare and they often run out of steam when tried.

Think long, go short: Justice, labour, and land issues are complicated and do not lend themselves readily to a traditional three-year project approach. Yet, reforms must provide tangible improvements fairly quickly to maintain the momentum for legal empowerment.

Support associations of the poor, but do not compromise their independence: The danger is that assisting these groups may cause them to become more accountable to the external funding agency than to their membership.

Dedicate resources to support participatory processes and coordination: While technical solutions often attract significant donor and government interest, capacity development for participation and coordination mechanisms is often undervalued and therefore under-funded.

Provide effective outreach: Without a dedicated promotion campaign, beneficiaries may not take advantage of reforms.

Provide access to information: Access to information helps people to better understand and advance their rights, for example in securing tenure or tackling job discrimination.

Use plain and local language: One of the key elements for national ownership of reform is language: dialogue, debate, and information sharing must be conducted in local languages, and legal documents demystified by reproducing them in layperson's terms.

Work with para-professionals: There are many opportunities to create a new generation of para-professionals who are trained and possibly certified to respond to the day-to-day service requirements of the poor. Para-professionals do not require the advanced studies of current professionals, which are often inappropriately scheduled, expensive, and include subjects of limited relevance to the prospective client base.

Bundle service delivery: This is a cost-effective strategy for delivering tangible benefits to the poor. One example is to deliver identity cards with vaccination programmes.

Be flexible. Take tactical advantage of opportunities as they arise and do not be constrained by a programmed calendar of deliverables.

largest global corporate-citizenship initiative, can play a central role in building support from the world of business, for systemic change for legal empowerment.

f) Initiative to promote grassroots knowledge and social innovation

The Commission recommends that a global initiative be launched to support the promotion of grass-roots knowledge and the spread of information about social innovations in the area of legal empowerment. Such an initiative should reach out broadly to the full range of organisations and networks in which poor people take part, from religious institutions to farmers' associations to women's networks. Recognition could come in many shapes, such as prizes, publications, funding, and technical support. This could be linked to the proposed Global Open Access Arena for Legal Empowerment.

g) Observance of an International Day for Legal Empowerment of the Poor

A special day for Legal Empowerment of the

Poor could be introduced to the UN Calendar of yearly observances. It would serve to promote Legal Empowerment of the Poor through local events worldwide, possibly emphasising the core rights of legal empowerment each year. In addition, it could highlight a particular theme closely related to legal empowerment.

Those who seek legal empowerment of poor people and communities will have the enduring admiration and support of this Commission, and of a daily-growing group of people and institutions that, after learning about the views presented in this report, come to share them. But much more important, they will earn the admiration of those whose lives they touch and have the satisfaction of helping to secure, amidst a multitude of desperate alternatives, a future of human flourishing.

Endnotes

In studies conducted on the ground in 20 countries since 1998 at the request of the governments of Guatemala, Bolivia, Panama, Honduras, Argentina, Mexico, Haiti, Dominican Republic, El Salvador, Ecuador, Colombia, Peru, Tanzania, Egypt, Albania, the Philippines, Ethiopia, Georgia, Ghana, and Pakistan, the Institute for Liberty and Democracy (ILD) conservatively estimated that between 70 percent and 90 percent of the urban and rural population were extralegal. Applying these results to 179 developing and former Soviet nations, according to the degree of development of their institutional framework, it was found that 85 percent of the population lived in extralegal areas. Given a population of 4.9 billion in these 179 countries, it was concluded that at least 4.1 billion live in extralegal areas.

Studies by a number of other organisations confirm this figure. The International Labour Organisation, in the 2002 edition of *Key Indicators of the* Labour *Market* estimated that 'more than 70 percent of the workforce in developing countries operates in the informal economy.' Taking into account the dependents of these workers, this means that at least 4.3 billion people in these countries rely on informal activities for their day-to-day subsistence. The World Bank Institute, using conventional definitions of under-employment and poverty, has come up with similar estimates. WBI organised the 'Inclusive and Sustainable Business: Opening Markets to the Poor' programme, with the objective of supporting strategies designed by private executives and public-sector leaders for creating opportunities 'for the world's four billion poor people.'

The ILD estimate has become an international standard, for example, a study supported by the Inter-American Development Bank, the International Finance Corporation, the World Bank Group, Microsoft, and the Shell Foundation, and A. Hammond's subsequent book *The Next 4 Billion: Market Size and Business Strategy at the Base of the Pyramid* (March 2007).

2   'Business rights' need not yet be regarded as a new term in law, but rather as derived from existing rights related to an individual doing business, newly bundled together under this term on the basis of the vital instrumentality of businesses in the livelihoods of the poor.

3   Schneider, Friedrich. 'Shadow Economies and Corruption all over the World: New Estimates for 145 Countries', July 2007, published in: Economics, The Open-Access, Open-Assessment E-Journal, No. 2007-9. Available at *http://www.econ.jku.at/Schneider/publik.html*

4   Low-income and rural populations often have difficulty accessing commercial banks. They may be illiterate, the local branch may be too far away, and fees and minimum balance requirements may be prohibitive. An estimated two billion people are without access to basic financial services. Figure based on DFID Press Release, 18 June 2007 *(http://www.dfid.gov.uk/News/files/pressreleases/bank-billion-benefit.asp)*.

5   DFID Press Release, 18 June 2007 *(http://www.dfid.gov.uk/News/files/pressreleases/bank-billion-benefit.asp)*

6   'Business rights' need not yet be regarded as a new term in law, but rather as derived from existing codified rights of the individual, newly bundled together under this term on the basis of their vital instrumentality in the livelihoods of the poor.

7   WDI 2007

8   The Millennium Development Goals Report 2007, UN, 2007.

9   World Bank: Economic Growth in the 1990s: Learning from a Decade of Reform, 2005.

10   North, D.C., Institutions, Institutional Change and Economic Performance. Cambridge: Cambridge University Press, 1990.

11   Stern, Dethier, and Rogers: Growth and Empowerment - Making Development Happen, MIT Press, 2005

12   Harmonising Donor Practices for Effective Aid Delivery Volume 2; DAC Guidelines and Reference Series; OECD-DAC 2006 *(http://www.oecd.org/dataoecd/53/7/34583142.pdf)*.

13   Thomas Carothers, Promoting the Rule of Law Abroad: The Problem of Knowledge, Carnegie Endowment Working Paper No. 34, Rule of Law Series, Democracy and Rule of Law Project, 3. Washington, D.C.: Carnegie Endowment for International Peace, January 2003.

14   According to the WDI 2007, there were an estimated 985 million people living in extreme poverty, i.e. living on less than one dollar a day in 2004. Some 500 million of those who survive on less than a dollar a day work, but despite their long hours of toil, in conditions that are often terrible, they cannot escape poverty. ILO, World Employment Report 2004-05; ILO, Working out of Poverty, 2003.

15   According to the WDI 2007, an estimated 2.6 billion people, almost half the population of the developing world, were still living below the poverty rate of two dollars a day.

16   See footnote 1.

17   Muhammad Yunus: 'Yunus takes microfinance to New York', Financial Times, 15 February 2008

18   World Bank (2007) Informality: Exit and Exclusion.

19   'Business rights' need not yet be regarded as a new term in law, but rather as derived from existing rights related to doing business of the individual, newly bundled together under this term on the basis of their vital instrumentality in the livelihoods of the poor.

20   Article 17, The Universal Declaration of Human Rights, UN Doc. G.A. res. 217A (III), U.N. Doc A/810at 71 (1948).

21   European Convention for the Protection of Human Rights and Fundamental Freedoms, (ETS No. 5), 213 U.N.T.S. 222, entered into force 3 September 1953, Protocol I on enforcement of certain rights and freedoms not included in Section I. of the Convention, 20 March 1952.

22   Article 21, American Convention on Human Rights, O.A.S. Treaty Series No. 36, 1144 U.N.T.S. 123 entered into force 18 July 1978, in: Basic Documents Pertaining to Human Rights in the Inter-American System, OEA/Ser.L.V/II.82 doc.6 rev.1 at 25 (1992).

23   Article 14, African [Banjul] Charter on Human and Peoples' Rights, adopted 27 June 1981, OAU Doc. CAB/LEG/67/3 rev. 5, 21 I.L.M. 58 (1982), entered into force 21 October 1986.

24   Economic and Social Council, Commission on Human Rights, Sub-Commission on the Promotion and Protection of Human Rights, 56th session, Economic, Social and Cultural Rights. 'Housing and property restitution in the context of the return of refugees and internally displaced persons'. Final report of the Special Rapporteur, Paulo Sérgio Pinheiro. E/CN.4/Sub.2/2005/1 28 June 2005. See Arts. 7; 15.

25   Available at http://www.everyhumanhasrights.org/read_it/ (25 January 2008). See esp. Arts. 2, 6, 7, 8, 17, 20, 23.

26   UNICEF. 2005. The 'Rights' Start to Life: A Statistical Analysis of Birth Registration, available at http://www.childinfo.org/areas/birthregistration/docs/Full%20text%20English.pdf. (23 January 2008)

27   Barendrecht, Maurits, Mulder, José and Giesen, Ivo, 'How to Measure the Price and Quality of Access to Justice?' (November 2006). http://ssrn.com/abstract=949209

28   Available at http://www.hrdc.net/sahrdc/hrfeatures/HRF154.htm and http://www.icj.org/news.php3?id_article=2684&lang=en

29   Available at http://allafrica.com/stories/200710021003.html and http://allafrica.com/stories/200708071187.html

30   American Bar Association, 'Judicial Reform Index for the Philippines', March 2006. Available at http://www.abanet.org/rol/publications/philippines_jri_2006.pdf

31   The five countries were Dominica, Grenada, Samoa, St. Lucia, and St. Vincent and the Grenadines, all tiny island states. Of the 76 countries measured within the CPIA, only Samoa scored an aggregate 4 out of 6 over the total 16 governance indicators. 2005 IDA Resource Allocation Index, available at www.worldbank.org

32   World Bank, CPIA 2005 Assessment Questionnaire: 33, available at www.worldbank.org

33   Available at http://www.ild.org.pe/en/whatwedo/diagnostics

34   Conditions are particularly severe in Africa, the Middle East and South Asia. See World Bank, Water Resources Sector Strategy: Strategic Directions for World Bank Engagement. World Bank, Washington D.C. (2003) p. 1

35   Available at http://www.icrw.org/. See also FAO 1999. 'Women's right to land and natural resources: some implications for a human rights based approach'. SD Dimensions. Available at: FAO: http://www.fao.org/sd/LTdirect/LTan0025.htm (23. January 2008).

36   ILO, Women and Men in the Informal Economy: A Statistical Picture, 2002

37   ILO, Resolution of the 90th Session of the General Conference, 2002

38   ILO: Working out of Poverty, 2003

39   Chen et al. 2005.

40   ILO, Women and Men in the Informal Economy: A Statistical Picture, 2002

41   ibid.

42   The informal economy of 96 developing countries accounts for 37 percent of the economy or official GDP. (Schneider, Friedrich. 'Shadow Economies and Corruption all over the World: New Estimates for 145 Countries', July 2007, published in: Economics, The Open-Access, Open-Assessment E-Journal, No. 2007-9. Available at http://www.econ.jku.at/Schneider/publik.html.

      The informal economy produces 27 percent of non-agricultural output in North Africa, 29 percent in Latin America and 31 percent in Sub-Saharan Africa and Asia. In Thailand and Nigeria, it exceeds 70 percent of the economy. (ILO, Women and Men in the Informal Economy: A Statistical Picture, 2002).

43   WRI Report 2005.

44   Boudreaux 2007.

45   HDR 2007/2008.

46   HDR 2007/2008. P Gutman 'From Goodwill to Payments for Environmental Services: A Survey of Financing Options for Sustainable Natural Resource Management in Developing Countries 2004.'

47   'Economic rent' is income that would not exist in a competitive marketplace. 'Rent-seeking' behaviour refers to efforts to get government to create economic rents, which can then be captured for private gain at the expense of society, due to the inefficiencies it creates.

48   De Soto, Hernando. 1989. The Other Path (New York: Basic Books).

49   Morton H. Halperin, Joseph T. Siegle, Michael M. Weinstein, 'The Democracy Advantage: How Democracies Promote Prosperity and Peace'. Routledge, 2005.

50   Journal of Democracy, July 2007, Volume 18, Number 3 (which is devoted to this debate and provides an overview including Snyder, Carothers, and Fukuyama).

51   Latin America: The Search for Good Jobs, Newsweek, 23 October 2007.

52   Dani Rodrik in Goodbye, Washington Consensus, Hello, Washington Confusion, Harvard, 2006 referring to Acemoglu, Johnson, and Robinson, 'The Colonial Origins of Comparative Development', American Economic Review, 2001.

53   2006 World Development Report: Equity and Development, September 2005.

54   Danielle Resnick and Regina Birner, Does Good Governance Contribute to Pro-poor Growth? A Conceptual Framework and Empirical Evidence from Cross-Country Studies, 2005.

55   World Development Indicators 2007.

56   World Bank. World Development Report 2005. A Better Investment Climate for Everyone. p.79.

57   Op. Cit. pp. 80-81.

58   Op. Cit. p. 80.

59   Galiani, Sebastián y Ernesto Schargrodsky. *Property Rights for the Poor: Effects of Land Titling.* En: Available at *http://economics.uchicago.edu/pdf/Galiani_022706.pdf.*

60   Field, Erica. *Property Rights and Investment in Urban Slums.* Available at *http://www.economics.harvard.edu/faculty/field/papers/FieldinvestJEEA.pdf.*

61   Field, Erica. 'Entitled to Work: Urban Property Rights and Labour Supply in Peru', page 24.

62   Ibid.

63   Place and Hazell 1993; Bruce and Migot-Adholla 1994; Harrison 1990; Mighot-Adholla et al. 1994a; Collier and Gunning 1999.

64   Article I of the Declaration of Philadelphia, 1944, Annex to the Constitution, Convention of the International Labour Organisation.

65   See Report of Working Group 3 in Chapter 3 of Volume II.

66   Resolution on decent work and the informal economy, ILO, 2002.

67   The term 'paralegal' may be somewhat misleading insofar as it suggests an assistant who performs ministerial legal tasks. Paralegals in many developing country programmes are better thought of as community activists who not only have a substantial training in legal principles, but also familiarity with local community norms and practices and an ability to offer advice and advocacy services that go beyond narrow legal advice.

68   Evidence from Angola, Brazil, Colombia, and other Latin American countries, Hungary, India, and South Africa on how this can be done is documented in *Courts and Social Transformation in New Democracies: An Institutional Voice for the Poor?* Eds. Roberto Gargella, Pilar Domingo, and Theunis Roux, Ashgate: U.K., 2007.

69   Brustinow 2006.

70   Outcome Document, paragraph 47. UN World Summit, New York, September 2005; ECOSOC Ministerial Declaration on Creating a conducive environment for productive employment and decent work, Geneva, July 2006;

71   See also Convention 156, Workers with Family Responsibilities.

72   No. 177, 1966.

73   ILD paper on Legal Tools to Empower Informal Businesses, submitted to WG4. 2006.

74   USAID, Removing Barriers to Formalization: The Case for Reform and Emerging Best Practice, 2005.

75   These international agreements include the Universal Declaration of Human Rights (UDHR), the International Covenant on Civil and Political Rights (ICCPR) and the International Covenant on Economic and Social Rights (ICESR), ILO Declaration on Fundamental Rights and Principles at work including fundamental core conventions on freedom of association and collective bargaining, and prohibition of forced labour, elimination of child labour and non-discrimination in promoting equality of opportunity and treatment, and the Indigenous and Tribal Peoples Convention, 1989 (ILO Convention No. 169). In addition, there is an internationally recognised 'Right to Adequate Housing', which includes security of tenure as one of its six components.

76   The full list of working groups is available in Volume II of this report.

77   Cotula 2007.

78   Two useful approaches to analysing stakeholder interests in development are DFID's drivers of change available at http://www.gsdrc.org/go/topic-guides/drivers-of-change, and SIDA's power analysis available at *http://www.sida.se/sida/jsp/sida.jsp?d=118&a=24300&language=en_US.*

79   Decker 2005.

80   Platteau 2004.

81   Interim report of the Special Representative of the Secretary-General on the issue of human rights and trans-national corporations and other business enterprises, E/CN.4/2006/97.

82   General Assembly resolution; A/RES/53/144.

Bibliography

African [Banjul] Charter on Human and Peoples' Rights. http://www1.umn.edu/humanrts/instree/z1afchar.htm.

American Bar Association. *Judicial Reform Index for the Philippines.* American Bar Association, March 2006. *http://www.abanet.org/ rol/publications/philippines_jri_2006.pdf.*

Barendrecht, Maurits, José Mulder, and Ivo Giesen. 'How to Measure the Price and Quality of Access to Justice,' November 2006. *http://papers.ssrn.com/sol3/Delivery.cfm/SSRN_ID949209_code74344.pdf?abstractid=949209&mirid=1.*

Boudreaux, Karol. *State Power, Entrepreneurship, and Coffee: The Rwandan Experience.* Mercatus Policy Series. *http://ssrn.com/ abstract=1026935.*

Bruce, John W., and S. E. Migot-Adholla. *Searching for Land Tenure Security in Africa.* Kendall/Hunt, 1994.

Brustinow, Angelika. '*Making Rights Work for the Poor; Alternative Dispute Resolution*' January 2006.

Chen, Martha. *Progress of the World's Women: Women, Work and Poverty.* United Nations Publications, 2005. *http://www.unifem.org/ attachments/products/PoWW2005_eng.pdf.*

Chen, Martha. *Women and Men in the Informal Economy: A statistical picture.* Geneva: ILO, 2002. *http://www.wiego.org/publications/ women%20and%20men%20in%20the%20informal%20economy.pdf.*

Collier, Paul. *The Bottom Billion: Why the poorest countries are failing and what can be done about it.* Oxford, New York: Oxford University Press, 2007.

Collier, Paul, and Jan Willem Gunning. 'Explaining African Economic Performance.' *Journal of Economic Literature* 37, no. 1. Journal of Economic Literature (1999): 64-111. *http://ideas.repec.org/a/aea/jeclit/v37y1999i1p64-111.html.*

Cotula, Lorenzo. *Changes in 'customary' Land Tenure Systems in Africa.* IIED, 2007.

Council of Europe. *Convention for the Protection of Human Rights and Fundamental Freedoms.* London: H. M. Stationery Off, 1951. *http://conventions.coe.int/treaty/en/Treaties/Html/005.htm.*

Crowley, Eve. 'FAO SD dimensions: Women's right to land and natural resources: Some implications for a human rights-based approach,' January 1999. *http://www.fao.org/sd/LTdirect/LTan0025.htm.*

Decker, Klaus, Caroline Sage, and Milena Stefanova. *Law or Justice: Building Equitable Legal Institutions.* World Bank, 2005. *http:// siteresources.worldbank.org/INTWDR2006/Resources/477383-1118673432908/Law_or_Justice_Building_Equitable_Legal_ Institutions.pdf.*

DFID News. Press Release, 'Billion benefit from bank accounts.' *http://www.dfid.gov.uk/News/files/pressreleases/bank-billion-benefit. asp.*

'Every Human Has Rights.' (Petition) *http://www.everyhumanhasrights.org/read_it/.*

Field, Erica. 'Entitled to Work: Urban Property Rights and Labor Supply in Peru.' *The Quarterly Journal of Economics* 122, no. 4. The Quarterly Journal of Economics (2007): 1561-1602. *http://ideas.repec.org/a/tpr/qjecon/v122y2007i4p1561-1602.html.*

Field, Erica. 'Property Rights and Investment in Urban Slums.' *Journal of the European Economic Association* 3, no. 2-3. Journal of the European Economic Association (2005): 279-290. *http://ideas.repec.org/a/tpr/jeurec/v3y2005i2-3p279-290.html.*

Galiani, Sebastian, and Ernesto Schargrodsky. *Property Rights for the Poor: Effects of Land Titling.* Universidad Torcuato Di Tella, 2005. RePEc. *http://ideas.repec.org/p/udt/wpbsdt/proprightspoor.html.*

Gargarella, Roberto. *Courts and social transformation in new democracies: an institutional voice for the poor?* Hampshire England, Burlington VT: Ashgate, 2006.

Halperin, Morton H., Joseph T. Siegle, and Michael M. Weinstein. *The Democracy Advantage: How Democracies Promote Prosperity and Peace.* Routledge, 2005.

Harrison, Paul. *Inside the Third World: The Anatomy of Poverty.* Penguin, 1990.

Harrison, Paul. *The Greening of Africa: Breaking Through in the Battle for Land and food.* New York N.Y. U.S.A.: Penguin, 1987.

He, Xin.'Why Do They Not Comply With the Law? Illegality and Semi-Legality Among Rural-Urban Migrant Entrepreneurs in Beijing.' *Law and Society Review* 39 (3), 527-562. 2005.

Human Rights Features (November 30, 2006). 'Legal Reforms and Investment Prospects in India'. *http://www.hrdc.net/sahrdc/hrfeatures/HRF154.htm.*

Inter-American Commission on Human Rights, and Inter-American Court of Human Rights. *Basic Documents Pertaining to Human Rights in the Inter-American System: Updated to 1 March 1988.* Washington, D.C: General Secretariat, Organization of American States, 1988. *http://www1.umn.edu/humanrts/oasinstr/zoas3con.htm.*

International Commission of Jurists. 'Attacks on Justice 2002 - India.' International Commission of Jurists, August 27, 2002. *http://www.icj.org/IMG/pdf/india.pdf.*

International Labour Office. *Working Out of Poverty: Report of the Director-General.* International Labour Organisation, 2003.

International Labour Organisation. 'Effect to be given to resolutions adopted by the International Labour Conference at its 90th Session (2002): (b) resolution concerning decent work and the informal economy.' *Papers of the Governing Body.* (2002). *http://www.ilo.org/public/english/standards/relm/gb/docs/gb285/pdf/gb-7-2.pdf.*

Journal of Democracy. Vol. 18. The Johns Hopkins University Press, 2007.

Langman, Jimmy. 'Latin America, The Search For Good Jobs.' *Newsweek*, December 22, 2003. *http://www.newsweek.com/id/60944.*

Machuhi, Eunice. 'Kenya: One Million Cases Pending in Courts'. *The Nation (Nairobi)*, August 7, 2007. *http://allafrica.com/stories/printable/200708071187.html.*

'Monitoring Elite Capture in Community-Driven Development.' *Development and Change* 35, no. 2 (April 2004): 223.

Muriuki, Albert. 'Slow Judicial System a Major Obstacle to Growth.' *Business Daily (Nairobi)*, October 2, 2007. http://allafrica.com/stories/printable/200710021003.html.

North, Douglass. *Institutions, Institutional Change and Economic Performance.* Cambridge University Press, 1990.

OECD DAC. *Harmonising Donor Practices for Effective Aid Delivery.* Vol. 2. DAC Guidelines and Reference Series. OECD Online Bookshop, 2006. *http://www.oecd.org/dataoecd/53/7/34583142.pdf.*

Perry, Guillermo, and William F. Maloney. *Informality: Exit and Exclusion.* World Bank Publications, 2007.

Pimlott, Daniel. 'Yunus takes microfinance to New York.' *Financial Times*, February 15, 2008. *http://www.ft.com/cms/s/0/f39adbe2-dc02-11dc-bc82-0000779fd2ac.html.*

Place, Frank, and Peter Hazell. 'Productivity Effects of Indigenous Land Tenure Systems in Sub-Saharan Africa.' *American Journal of Agricultural Economics* Vol. 75, No. 1 (February 1993): 10-19.

Resnick, Danielle, and Regina Birner. *Does Good Governance Contribute to Pro-poor Growth? A Conceptual Framework and Empirical Evidence from Cross-Country Studies.* Verein fuer Socialpolitik, Research Committee Development Economics. 2005. *http://ideas.repec.org/p/zbw/gdec05/3478.html.*

Rodrik, Dani. 'Washington Consensus, Hello, Washington Confusion,' January 2006. *http://ksghome.harvard.edu/~drodrik/Lessons%20of%20the%201990s%20review%20_JEL_.pdf.*

Ruiz-Restrepo, Adriana 'Broadening Access to Organizations of the Poor: Strengthening NPOs through Constitutional Justice' Global Network of Government Innovators, Ash Institute at John F. Kennedy School of Government, Harvard University, November 2007, The Hague, Netherlands. *www.innovations.harvard.edu.*

Schneider, Friedrich. 'Shadow Economies and Corruption All Over the World: New Estimates for 145 Countries.' *The Open-Access, Open-Assessment E-Journal* Vol. 1, 2007-9 (July 24, 2007). *http://www.economics-ejournal.org/economics/journalarticles/2007-9.*

Smith, Stirling. and Ross, Cilla., 'Organizing out of poverty: stories from the grassroots: How the SYNDICOOP approach has worked in East Africa', ILO, International Cooperative Alliance and the International Confederation of Free Trade Unions, 2006.

Soto, Hernando de. *The Other Path: The Economic Answer to Terrorism.* 1st Perseus Books Group, 2002.

Soto, Hernando de. *The Mystery of Capital: Why Capitalism Triumphs in the West and Fails Everywhere Else.* New York: Basic Books, 2000.

Stern, Nicholas Herbert, J-J Dethier, and F. Halsey Rogers. *Growth and Empowerment: Making Development Happen.* MIT Press, 2005.

UN Economic and Social Council. *http://www.un.org/ecosoc/docs/fullandp10.shtml.*